Cargo Securement Handbook for Drivers

©2007

First Edition, Sixth Printing, December 2007

J. J. Keller & Associates, Inc.
3003 W. Breezewood Lane, P.O. Box 368
Neenah, Wisconsin 54957-0368
USA
Phone: (800) 327-6868
Fax: (800) 727-7516
www.jjkeller.com
Library of Congress Catalog Card Number: 2005920968
ISBN 1-59042-610-X

Canadian Goods and Services Tax (GST) Number: R123-317687

Printed in the U.S.A.

All rights reserved. Neither the publication nor any part thereof may be reproduced in any manner without written permission of the Publisher. United States laws and Federal regulations published as promulgated are in public domain. However, their compilation and arrangement along with other materials in this publication are subject to the copyright notice.

DRIVER'S RECEIPT

I acknowledge receipt of this **Cargo Securement Handbook for Drivers**, which covers the following securement topics:

- General Cargo Securement Requirements
- Commodity-Specific Securement Requirements
- Frequently Asked Questions
- CVSA Out-of-Service Criteria for Cargo Securement
- Cargo Securement Regulations
- U.S. Manufacturing Standards
- Default Working Load Limits for Unmarked Tiedowns
- Tiedown Quick Reference
- Glossary

_____

Employee's Signature   Date

_____

Company

_____

Company Supervisor's Signature

NOTE: This receipt shall be read and signed by the employee. A responsible company supervisor shall countersign the receipt and place it in the employee's training file.

Disclaimer Notice

Due to the constantly changing nature of technology and best practices it is impossible to guarantee the applicability of the content contained herein to any particular situation. Reference to any product is not an endorsement of that product or its manufacturer.

Use of the information in this publication is the sole responsibility of the user. J. J. Keller & Associates, Inc., ("Keller") expressly disclaims any and all warranties or guarantees of any kind whatsoever, either expressed or implied, including without limitation any warranties of merchantability or fitness for a particular purpose. In no event will Keller be liable for any incidental, special, exemplary, punitive, indirect or consequential damages arising out of or relating in any way to use of the content including without limitation, lost savings, lost profits, civil or criminal forfeitures.

Keller does not assume any responsibility for omissions, errors, misprint, or ambiguity in the content and shall not be held liable by such.

The content may help motor carrier personnel better understand how to secure different types of cargo. J. J. Keller assumes no liability for reliance on this content or use thereof. The content does not constitute a standard, specification, or regulation. The individual(s) securing the load ultimately takes responsibility for cargo and load securement.

Table of Contents

1. INTRODUCTION 1
2. GENERAL CARGO SECUREMENT REQUIREMENTS 3
   2.1 The Fundamentals of Cargo Securement 3
   2.2 The Securement System and its Components 9
   2.3 Containing, Immobilizing, and Securing Cargo 19
   2.4 Inspection Requirements 37
3. COMMODITY-SPECIFIC SECUREMENT REQUIREMENTS 39
   3.1 Logs 39
   3.2 Dressed Lumber and Similar Building Materials 49
   3.3 Metal Coils 57
   3.4 Paper Rolls 69
   3.5 Concrete Pipe 83
   3.6 Intermodal Containers 95
   3.7 Automobiles, Light Trucks, and Vans 99
   3.8 Heavy Vehicles, Equipment, and Machinery 101
   3.9 Flattened or Crushed Vehicles 109
   3.10 Roll-On/Roll-Off and Hook-Lift Containers 113

Table of Contents

- 3.11 Boulders 117
- 3.12 Square Bales of Hay and Straw 125
- 4. REFERENCE 129
  - 4.1 Frequently Asked Questions (FAQs) 129
  - 4.2 CVSA North American Standard Vehicle Out-of-Service Criteria: Cargo Securement 131
  - 4.3 Cargo Securement Regulations 137
  - 4.4 U.S. Manufacturing Standards 167
  - 4.5 Default Working Load Limits for Unmarked Tiedowns 169
  - 4.6 Tiedown Quick Reference 173
  - 4.7 Glossary 175

1. INTRODUCTION

Keller's *Cargo Securement Handbook for Drivers* is a field guide and reference for securing cargo on commercial motor vehicles according to the standards in effect in both the United States and Canada. The *Handbook* will help you to:

- Stay in compliance with U.S. and Canadian cargo securement regulations.
- Safely load and secure various types of commodities.
- Inspect a secured load for compliance with U.S. and Canadian regulations.

 Where a difference exists between U.S. and Canadian rules, the Canadian differences will be noted, with a maple leaf providing a visual cue.

Local regulations may be more or less stringent, so be sure to check your state, provincial, and local laws too.

 Important regulatory and best-practices information will be highlighted throughout the text, like this.

What's included in this handbook?

Chapters 2.1 through 2.4 of this handbook cover general cargo securement and inspection requirements that apply to most commodities hauled by commercial motor vehicle. This is where to turn first for information about the basic securement requirements.

Chapters 3.1 through 3.12 discuss the securement of specific types of commodities, from logs to boulders to hook-lift containers, as addressed in the cargo securement regulations.

 When hauling one of the specific commodities addressed in section 3, you must comply with both the "general" securement regulations covered in section 2 <u>and</u> the commodity-specific regulations discussed in section 3. If there is a conflict between the general and cargo-specific rules, you must comply with the more stringent (tougher) requirement.

1. INTRODUCTION

In the REFERENCE section of the handbook, chapter 4.1 contains Frequently Asked Questions (FAQs) about cargo securement, and chapter 4.2 contains a list of the securement violations that can place a vehicle out of service (from the CVSA's Out-of-Service Criteria).

Chapter 4.3 contains the U.S. cargo inspection and securement regulations, as well as information on viewing or obtaining the Canadian standards.

Chapters 4.4 through 4.6 contain reference charts for:

1. U.S. manufacturing standards for securement devices,
2. Working load limits for unmarked tiedowns, and
3. Determining the number of chains and straps needed to secure a given weight of cargo, based on working load limits and cargo weight alone.

Finally, chapter 4.7 contains a glossary of commonly used terms.

2. GENERAL CARGO SECUREMENT REQUIREMENTS
2.1 The Fundamentals of Cargo Securement

- Why is cargo securement so important? ... 3
- The rules ... 4
- Which vehicles are covered? ... 4
- What are the essential requirements? ... 5
- How well must the securement system work? ... 7

The guiding principle of cargo securement is that cargo being transported on public roads must remain secured on or within the transporting vehicle. Proper cargo securement prevents cargo from shifting or leaking, spilling, blowing, or falling from the vehicle.

A properly secured load will remain secured:

- Under all conditions that could reasonably be expected to occur in normal driving; and
- When you are responding to an emergency situation (except when there is a crash).

Why is cargo securement so important?

An improperly secured load can result in:

- Vehicle accidents.
- Loss of life.
- Loss of load.
- Damage to the cargo.
- Damage to vehicles and other property.

2.1 The Fundamentals of Cargo Securement

- Issuance of citations/fines to you and/or your company.
- Higher insurance rates.
- Your vehicle being placed out of service.

The rules

Cargo securement isn't just a good idea — it's required.

- In the U.S, you must follow the rules in 49 CFR Part 393, Subpart I, *Protection Against Shifting and Falling Cargo*.
- In Canada, you must comply with National Safety Code Standard 10, *Cargo Securement,* and provincial standards.

These regulations are both based on the *North American Cargo Securement Standard*, designed to harmonize and improve the securement practices across North America.

Which vehicles are covered?

The standards apply to commercial motor vehicles, including vehicle combinations, that are operated on a highway and either:

1. Have a gross vehicle weight rating (GVWR), gross combination weight rating (GCWR), gross vehicle weight (GVW) or gross combination weight (GCW) of 10,001 pounds (4,536 kg) or more, whichever is greater; OR

2. Are used in transporting hazardous materials in a quantity requiring placarding under the U.S. Hazardous Materials Regulations.

2.1 The Fundamentals of Cargo Securement

In Canada, the securement standards in NSC Standard 10 apply to vehicles with a gross vehicle rating over 4,500 kg (10,000 lb.)

This includes <u>any</u> cargo and dangerous goods or hazardous materials, including:

- All general freight, including freight transported in enclosed trailers.
- All equipment carried for vehicle operation, such as chains, dollies, tires, blocks, etc.
- Intermodal containers and their contents.

Some specific commodities have additional or different securement requirements, and will be covered in section 3 of this handbook.

Additional requirements under separate regulations may also apply for transportation of certain types of dangerous goods or hazardous materials.

It is assumed that heavy loads carried under special permits would be subject to securement standards contained in the special permit, which may differ from federal standards. Check with your federal, provincial, or state government for any permit requirements.

What are the essential requirements?

Before you can operate a commercial motor vehicle, and before your company can require or permit you to operate a commercial motor vehicle, you must be certain that the vehicle's cargo and equipment are properly secured.

- The vehicle's cargo must be properly distributed and adequately secured.
- The vehicle's structure and equipment must be secured, including:
  - Tailgate
  - Doors
  - Tarpaulins
  - Spare tire
  - Other equipment used in the vehicle's operation
  - Cargo securing equipment

2.1 The Fundamentals of Cargo Securement

- The cargo or any other object must not:
    - Obscure the driver's view ahead or to the right or left sides (except for drivers of self-steer dollies).
    - Interfere with the free movement of the driver's arms or legs.
    - Prevent the driver's free and ready access to accessories required for emergencies.
    - Prevent the free and ready exit of any person from the vehicle's cab or driver's compartment.

 Refer to chapter 2.4 for load securement inspection requirements.

All cargo must be contained, immobilized, or secured so that it does not:

- Leak,
- Spill,
- Blow off the vehicle,
- Fall from the vehicle,
- Fall through the vehicle,

- Otherwise become dislodged from the vehicle, or
- Shift upon or within the vehicle to such an extent that the vehicle's stability or maneuverability is adversely affected.

 There can be some movement if it doesn't reduce the effectiveness of the securement system.

2.1 The Fundamentals of Cargo Securement

How well must the securement system work?

Each cargo securement system must be able to withstand a minimum amount of force in each direction, as follows:

- **Forward Force** — 80% of cargo weight when braking while driving straight ahead.
- **Rearward Force** — 50% of cargo weight when accelerating, shifting gears while climbing a hill, or braking in reverse.
- **Sideways Force** — 50% of cargo weight when turning, changing lanes, or braking while turning.
- **Upward Force** — 20% of cargo weight when traveling over bumps in the road or cresting a hill, unless cargo is fully contained within the structure of the vehicle.

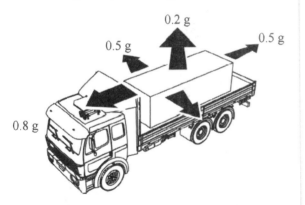

 The above forces represent "extreme" conditions just short of a crash. Under normal, day-to-day operating conditions, you have to make sure the *working load limit* of the system is not exceeded under a:
- Forward force of 44% of the cargo weight,
- Rearward force of 50% of the cargo weight, and
- Sideways force of 25% of the cargo weight.

 Canada does not distinguish between "extreme" operating conditions and "normal" operating conditions. The securement system must withstand the "extreme" forces above at all times.

2.1 The Fundamentals of Cargo Securement

 When referring to these forces, the regulations refer to the "g" force. This force can be thought of as the force of gravity in relation to the cargo weight. So "0.5 g" is 50% of the force of gravity or 50% of the cargo weight.

As a driver, you should be aware that these "force" standards exist in the regulations, but fortunately you are not expected to apply them on a routine basis. As discussed later in this handbook, your securement system will meet these performance requirements if your cargo is fully contained or immobilized. The regulations allow you to determine a cargo securement method based on the weight of the cargo and the rated strength of the securement devices rather than the forces being applied.

2.2 The Securement System and its Components

Which vehicle structures are included? ... 10
How strong do the vehicle structure and anchor points have to be? 10
What is a securing device? 11
What is a tiedown? 11
Tiedown construction and maintenance .. 12
Selecting a tiedown 13
Tiedown use 15
Edge protection 15
Blocking and bracing 16
Front end structures in contact with cargo 17

A *securement system* is a securement method that uses one or a combination of the following elements:

1. Vehicle structures, such as anchor points and headerboards.
2. Securing devices, such as steel straps, wires, chains, rope, and ratchets.
3. Blocking and bracing equipment, such as wood blocks and shoring bars.

2.2 The Securement System and its Components

The securement system chosen must be appropriate for the cargo's size, shape, strength, and characteristics. The articles of cargo should have sufficient structural integrity to withstand the forces of loading, securement, and transportation. This includes packaged articles, unitized articles, and articles stacked one on the other.

Which vehicle structures are included?

- Floors
- Walls
- Decks
- Tiedown anchor points
- Headerboards
- Bulkheads
- Stakes
- Posts
- Mounting pockets
- Anchor points

Generally, the cab shield is not part of the cargo securement system. However, a headerboard, bulkhead, or other front-end structure can be used to provide restraint against forward movement if the cargo is in contact with it and it meets federal specifications (addressed later in this chapter).

How strong do the vehicle structure and anchor points have to be?

All elements of the vehicle structure and anchor points must be strong enough to withstand the forces described in chapter 2.1:

- Forward force: 0.8 g (80%)
- Rearward force: 0.5 g (50%)
- Sideways force: 0.5 g (50%)
- Upward force: 0.2 g (20%)

Alternate criteria for front end structures will be addressed later in this chapter.

2.2 The Securement System and its Components

All anchor points and elements of the vehicle structure must be in good working order, with:

- No obvious damage (including cracks or cuts) that would adversely affect performance or reduce the working load limit.
- No distress.
- No weakened parts or sections.

What is a securing device?

A securing device is any device specifically manufactured to attach or secure cargo to a vehicle or trailer. This includes:

- Friction mats
- Chain
- Wire rope
- Manila rope
- Synthetic rope
- Binders
- Shackles
- Winches
- Stake pockets
- D-rings
- Steel strapping
- Clamps and latches
- Blocking
- Front-end structure
- Grab hooks
- Pockets
- Webbing ratchets
- Bracing
- Synthetic webbing
- Binders

What is a tiedown?

A tiedown is a combination of securing devices that forms an assembly that:

- Attaches cargo to, or restrains cargo on a vehicle or trailer.
- Is attached to anchor point(s).

Some tiedowns are attached directly to the cargo or have both tiedown ends attached to the same side of the vehicle, providing direct resistance to external forces. These are called *direct tiedowns*.

2.2 The Securement System and its Components

Direct tiedowns attach to cargo

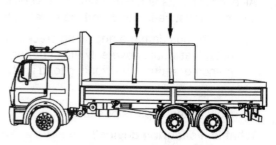

Indirect tiedowns pass over or through cargo

Some tiedowns pass over or through the cargo, creating a downward force that increases the effect of friction between the cargo and the deck, thereby restraining the cargo. These are called *indirect tiedowns*. In many cases, this friction between the load and deck is the principal factor affecting load securement (although friction alone is never enough to secure a load).

Tiedown construction and maintenance

Tiedowns and/or their associated connectors or attachment mechanisms (except for steel strapping) must be designed, constructed, and maintained so that the driver can tighten them.

All components of each tiedown must be in proper working order, with no defects that reduce the working load limit:

- No knots, cracks, cuts, or other obvious damage that would adversely affect performance.

2.2 The Securement System and its Components

- No distress.
- No weakened parts.
- No weakened sections.

Finally, tiedown assemblies (including chains, wire rope, steel strapping, synthetic webbing, and cordage) and other attachment or fastening devices used to secure cargo must comply with the manufacturing standards listed in chapter 4.5, *U.S. Manufacturing Standards.*

Selecting a tiedown

Selecting the type of tiedown to use is often a matter of personal choice, but some tiedowns just work better for certain types of loads (and in certain cases, the rules specify which type to use).

- **Chain** — The strongest and most durable tiedown, chain is required for some items (like boulders) but may be too heavy for others. When using chain:

  - Make sure your chains, anchor points, *and binders* have a high enough rating for the weight of the cargo.

  - Use extreme caution with binders: position them so you pull *down* on the handle, and never be in a position such that you could be struck by the handle.

> Inspect your chain <u>links</u> for gouges, cuts, chips, abrasion, bends, and twists. Use only approved repair links (such as clevis-type) to repair chains.
>
> On <u>binders</u>, check for worn pins, bent tongues, open or bent hooks, bent couplers, bent eye bolts, and badly worn threads.

  - Install chains carefully so they are free of twists and the links set up in a stable manner.

  - Make sure there are no kinks, snags, or hang-ups in long chain spans — these can lead to a loss of tension.

2.2 The Securement System and its Components

- Use your own strength to tension lever-type and ratchet binders. Do not use a pipe or other device ("cheater bar") to extend the lever and tension the tiedown beyond its limits.

- **Strapping** — Synthetic straps are ideal for securing small loads, loads in enclosed trailers, and heavier loads. They are not as durable or strong as chain and are susceptible to chafing. When using straps:

  - Make sure the straps, hooks, and tensioning devices are strong enough for the cargo, and not damaged.

  - Check for knots, crushed areas, cuts, burns, holes, splices, severe abrasion, and broken load-bearing strands. (Refer to the Out-of-Service Criteria for standards that must be met.)

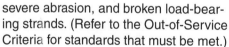

- Use edge protectors when required, to protect the straps.

 Webbing cannot be repaired or spliced, so extra care is needed. If possible, store straps inside, off their spools, when not used for an extended period of time.

- **Rope** — Rope is used to secure cotton, hay, scrap paper bales, and similar types of loads, or may be used in addition to other types of tiedowns. Also used for tarps and other cargo covers. Rope can be affected by moisture and/or sunlight and can break down with use. When using rope, watch for burned or melted fibers (except on heat-sealed ends), excessive wear, and knots. Know the rated strength when possible!

- **Wire rope** — Wire rope is much stronger than natural or synthetic rope, but is less flexible. It is sometimes used when a chain is impractical.

2.2 The Securement System and its Components

- **Steel strapping** — Used to secure boxes, crates, and cartons, or for securing these items to pallets. While strong, steel strapping:
  - Can be snapped by vibration;
  - Cannot be adjusted without a special tool;
  - Must be carefully protected from sharp edges, to avoid crimping;
  - Must have two seals on end-over-end lap joints, and two pairs of crimps for each seal if wider than one inch.

Tiedown use

Each tiedown must be attached and secured so that it does not become loose or unfastened, open, or release during transit.

Because rub rails are designed to protect the securement system, tiedowns and other securement components used on a vehicle equipped with rub rails should be located behind (inboard of) the rub rails, whenever possible, though this is not required in the U.S.

 In Canada, securement devices MUST be routed inboard of the rub rails whenever "practical." Rub rails can be used as anchor points if the tiedown is fitted with a flat hook end and it is not possible to attach the hook to another more suitable anchor point.

Edge protection

Edge protection must be used if a tiedown could be cut or torn when touching an article of cargo. This is especially important for potentially abrasive or sharp cargo, like bricks and steel. The edge protection itself must also resist crushing, cutting, and abrasion.

2.2 The Securement System and its Components

Edge protection is also useful for protecting cargo or dunnage that is much softer than the tiedown, to prevent damage from crushing.

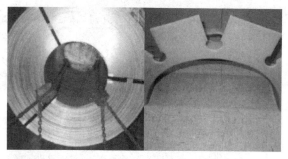

Blocking and bracing

The material used for blocking or bracing and as chocks and cradles must be strong enough to withstand being split or crushed by the cargo or tiedowns.

This requirement also applies to any material used for dunnage ("dunnage" is any loose material used to support and protect cargo).

If wood is used:

- Hardwood is recommended.
- It should be properly seasoned.
- It should be free from rot or decay, knots, knotholes, and splits.
- The grain should run lengthwise when using wood for blocking or bracing.

- When using blocking, use new nails whenever possible, and pound them straight through the block (perpendicular to the deck) until the head contacts the block. At least $1^{1}/_{4}$ inches of nail should penetrate into the deck.

- Don't leave clearance between the block and the cargo, and place blocks on all sides of the cargo.

- Replace damaged or splintered blocks and deck boards.

- Blocking should not be relied upon as a significant contributor to the securement of heavy cargo. Keep this in mind: A typical 16d nail through a softwood 2x4 has a WLL of only about 300 pounds.

2.2 The Securement System and its Components

Front end structures in contact with cargo

Special performance requirements apply when your cargo is in contact with the front end structure. The front end structure must meet the following performance requirements:

- **Height**: At least 4 feet (122 cm) above the floor of the vehicle, OR lower as long as it blocks forward movement of any cargo on the vehicle.
- **Width**: As wide as the vehicle, OR narrower as long as it blocks forward movement of any cargo on the vehicle.

- **Strength**: It must be capable of withstanding the following horizontal forward static load:
  - For a front end structure less than 6 feet (1.83 m) tall, a horizontal forward static load equal to 50% of the weight of the cargo when the cargo is uniformly distributed over the entire portion of the front end structure that is within 4 feet above the vehicle's floor (or at or below a height above the vehicle's floor at which it blocks forward movement of the cargo, if lower); OR
  - For a front end structure 6 feet (1.83 m) tall or taller, a horizontal forward static load equal to 40% of the weight of the cargo when the cargo is uniformly distributed over the entire front end structure.

2.2 The Securement System and its Components

- **Penetration resistance**: It must be designed, constructed, and maintained so that it is capable of resisting penetration by any article of cargo that contacts it when the vehicle decelerates at a rate of 20 feet (6.1 m) per second, per second.
    - It must have no openings large enough to allow any article of cargo in contact with the structure to pass through it.

 You may use an alternate device that performs the same functions as a front end structure as long as the device is at least as strong as, and provides protection against shifting articles of cargo at least equal to, a front end structure which conforms to the above requirements.

2.3 Containing, Immobilizing, and Securing Cargo

Cargo-specific rules 19
Three ways to transport cargo 20
Loading the cargo properly 23
How many tiedowns do I need? 25
How should tiedowns be attached? 27
Tiedown placement 28
Direct tiedowns 28
Indirect tiedowns 30
What about low-friction situations? 31
Tiedown strength and working load limits . 31
Working load limits: unmarked components 32
Working load limits: marked components . 33
Aggregate working load limit 34
How do you calculate the aggregate WLL? 34
What should the aggregate WLL be? 35
Putting it all together 36

The rules for containing, immobilizing, and securing cargo apply to all types of cargo EXCEPT:

- Commodities in bulk that lack structure or fixed shape (for example, liquids, gases, grain, sand, gravel, aggregate, liquid concrete).

- Commodities that are transported in the structure of a commercial motor vehicle such as a tank, hopper, or box.

Cargo-specific rules

The rules contain specific securement requirements for certain types of loads. When transport-

2.3 Containing, Immobilizing, and Securing Cargo

ing these commodities, you must use the specific requirements for that commodity as addressed in section 3.

- Logs
- Dressed lumber and similar building products
- Metal coils
- Paper rolls
- Concrete pipe loaded crosswise on a platform vehicle
- Intermodal containers
- Automobiles, light trucks, and vans
- Heavy vehicles, equipment, and machinery
- Flattened or crushed vehicles
- Roll-on/roll-off and hook-lift containers
- Large boulders

The commodity-specific securement rules take precedence over the "general" securement requirements for the cargo listed above when *additional* requirements are given for those commodities.

Three ways to transport cargo

All types of cargo must meet one of three conditions:

- Condition 1 — Cargo is **fully contained** by structures of adequate strength.
    - Cargo cannot shift or tip to such an extent that vehicle stability or handling is adversely affected.
    - Cargo is restrained against horizontal movement by vehicle structures (such as walls) or by other cargo. Horizontal movement includes forward, rearward, and side-to-side.

2.3 Containing, Immobilizing, and Securing Cargo

If the cargo is contained in a sided vehicle, the vehicle structure must be strong enough to withstand the forces described in chapter 2.1:

- Forward force: 0.8 g (80%)
- Rearward force: 0.5 g (50%)
- Sideways force: 0.5 g (50%)

Your personal safety is at stake if loose articles are not contained within the trailer. The cargo could shift during transportation and end up resting against the doors. When you unlatch the doors or open them, the cargo could fall out, and onto you.

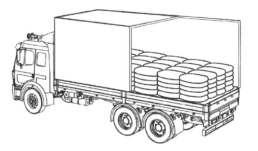

2.3 Containing, Immobilizing, and Securing Cargo

- Condition 2 — Cargo is **immobilized by structures** of adequate strength or a combination of structure, blocking, and bracing to prevent shifting or tipping to such an extent that vehicle stability or handling is adversely affected.

- Condition 3 — To prevent shifting or tipping, cargo is **immobilized or secured on or within a vehicle** by tiedowns along with:
  - Blocking
  - Bracing
  - Friction mats
  - Other cargo
  - Void fillers
  - A combination of these

2.3 Containing, Immobilizing, and Securing Cargo

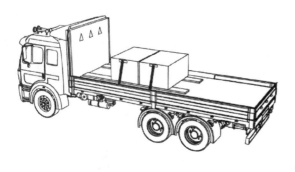

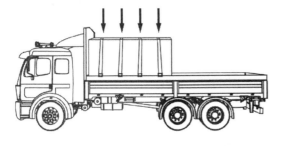

Loading the cargo properly

For articles of cargo placed beside each other and secured by side-to-side (transverse) tiedowns, either:

- Place them in direct contact with each other, OR

- Prevent them from shifting towards each other in transit by using blocking or by filling the space with other cargo. Vehicle motion can cause cargo to compress and fill any open spaces, thereby causing the tiedowns to become loose.

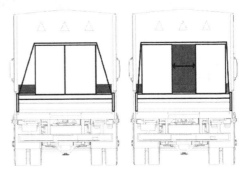

2.3 Containing, Immobilizing, and Securing Cargo

Some articles have a tendency to roll. To prevent rolling, provide more than one point of contact:

- Lift the cargo off the deck; AND/OR
- Use chocks, wedges, a cradle, or other equivalent means to prevent rolling. These **must** be secured to the deck.

The method used to prevent rolling must not become unfastened or loose while the vehicle is in transit.

For articles that have a tendency to tip, prevent tipping or shifting by bracing the cargo. A "brace" is a structure, device, or another substantial article placed against an article of cargo to prevent it from tipping. Braces may also help prevent cargo from shifting.

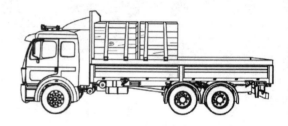

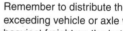 Remember to distribute the load evenly to avoid exceeding vehicle or axle weight limits, and keep the heaviest freight on the bottom.

2.3 Containing, Immobilizing, and Securing Cargo

How many tiedowns do I need?

When tiedowns are used as part of a cargo securement system, the number of tiedowns needed depends on:

1. Whether the cargo is prevented from moving forward,
2. The length and weight of the cargo, AND
3. The strength of the tiedowns.

The **minimum** number of tiedowns needed depends on the first two factors. Additional tiedowns must be added, however, when the minimum number of tiedowns is not enough, based on their strength, to secure the cargo adequately.

This section will tell you the **minimum** number of tiedowns needed, while tiedown strength will be addressed later in this handbook.

 Go beyond the minimum: provide some redundancy so the cargo remains secure even if one component of the securement system fails.

If cargo **is not prevented** from forward movement (for example, by the headerboard, bulkhead, other cargo, or tiedowns attached to the cargo), secure the cargo according to the following requirements:

If the article is:	use at least:
• 5 feet (1.52 m) or shorter, AND • 1,100 pounds (500 kg) or lighter	1 tiedown

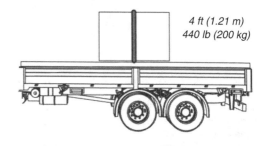

4 ft (1.21 m)
440 lb (200 kg)

25

2.3 Containing, Immobilizing, and Securing Cargo

If the article is:	use at least:
• 5 feet (1.52 m) or shorter, AND • over 1,100 pounds (500 kg)	2 tiedowns

If the article is:	use at least:
longer than 10 feet (3.04 m)	2 tiedowns, plus 1 additional tiedown for every additional 10 feet (3.04 m) or part thereof

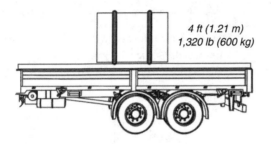

4 ft (1.21 m)
1,320 lb (600 kg)

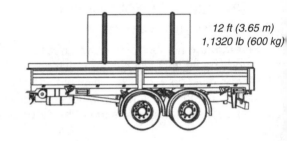

12 ft (3.65 m)
1,1320 lb (600 kg)

If the article is:	use at least:
longer than 5 feet (1.52 m) but is 10 feet (3.04 m) or less, no matter what the weight is	2 tiedowns

2.3 Containing, Immobilizing, and Securing Cargo

When cargo **is prevented** from forward movement (for example, by the headerboard, bulkhead, other cargo, or tiedowns), secure the cargo according to the following requirements:

If the article is:	use at least:
prevented from moving forward	1 tiedown for every 10 feet (3.04 m) or part thereof

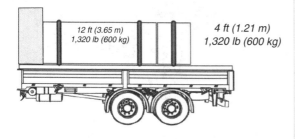

12 ft (3.65 m)
1,320 lb (600 kg)

4 ft (1.21 m)
1,320 lb (600 kg)

How should tiedowns be attached?

Tiedowns can be used in two ways. They can be:

1. Attached to the cargo or pull the cargo in only one direction ("direct" tiedowns)

    - Tiedowns are attached to an anchor point on the vehicle and then attached directly to the cargo, OR
    - Tiedowns are attached to an anchor point on the vehicle, passed over, through, or around the cargo, and then attached back to the same side of the vehicle.

2. Passed over the cargo ("indirect" tiedowns)

    - Tiedowns are attached to the vehicle, passed over, through, or around the cargo, and then attached to the vehicle again on the other side.

 Exception: other methods may be needed for articles of cargo such as machinery or fabricated structural items (e.g., steel or concrete beams, crane booms, girders, and trusses, etc.) which, because of their design, size, shape, or weight, must be fastened by special methods.

2.3 Containing, Immobilizing, and Securing Cargo

Tiedown placement

Unless the cargo prevents it, tiedowns should be positioned as symmetrically as possible over the length of the article(s). Position the tiedowns to preserve the integrity of the article(s).

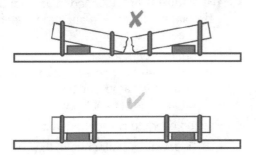

When spacers are used, tiedowns should be placed as close as possible to the spacers.

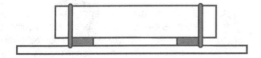

Direct tiedowns

Tiedowns attached to the cargo, or with both ends attached to the same side of the vehicle, work by counteracting the forces acting on the cargo.

When possible, the angle where the tiedown attaches to the vehicle should be shallow, not deep (ideally less than 45°).

To counteract **forward** movement, attach the tiedown so it pulls the cargo toward the rear of the vehicle.

2.3 Containing, Immobilizing, and Securing Cargo

To counteract **rearward** movement, attach the tiedown so it pulls the cargo toward the front of the vehicle.

To counteract movement **to one side**, attach the tiedown so it pulls the cargo toward the opposite side of the vehicle.

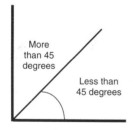

2.3 Containing, Immobilizing, and Securing Cargo

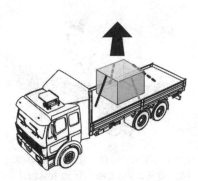

To counteract **upward** movement, attach tiedowns to opposing sides of the cargo so they pull the cargo down.

Indirect tiedowns

Tiedowns that pass over the cargo, with ends attached to opposite sides of the vehicle, work by increasing the effective weight of the cargo (they make the cargo seem heavier). This increases the pressure of the cargo on the deck and keeps the cargo from shifting.

Tension these tiedowns to as high an initial tension as possible.

The steeper the tiedown angle, the less shifting (ideally, the angle should be more than 45°).

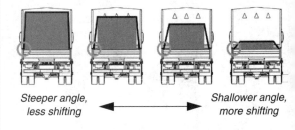

Steeper angle, less shifting ⟷ *Shallower angle, more shifting*

2.3 Containing, Immobilizing, and Securing Cargo

What about low-friction situations?

When there is low friction between the cargo and the deck (for example, with snow, ice, sand, gravel, or oil):

- Use tiedowns attached to the cargo (direct tiedowns), OR
- Use a means to improve the friction such as friction mats or tiedowns that pass over the cargo, OR
- Use blocking and tiedowns.

- Friction mats can greatly increase friction, so their use is encouraged.
- If the outside of your cargo is dirty or oily, clean it to maximize friction between cargo and tiedowns.

Tiedown strength and working load limits

The "working load limit" (WLL) is the maximum load that may be applied to a component of a cargo securement system during normal service. Apply a heavier load, and the component could break.

The WLL is usually assigned by the component manufacturer, and may or may not be marked on the component.

As the saying goes, a chain is only as strong as its weakest link, and this principle applies to all tiedowns and their load limits. The WLL for a

2.3 Containing, Immobilizing, and Securing Cargo

tiedown is the lowest WLL of any of its parts (including the tensioner) or the WLL of the anchor points it is attached to, whichever is less.

Every device contributes to the WLL of the securement system.

Canadian standards specify that the WLL of all components used to block cargo from forward movement must be 50% (or more) of the weight of the article being blocked.

If your tiedowns have even 1 inch (2-3 cm) of slack, the hooks could fall out. Whenever possible, attach hooks so that gravity holds them in place should the tiedown become slack.

Working load limits: unmarked components

Any securing device that is not marked by the manufacturer is considered to have a WLL as specified in chapter 4.6, Default Working Load Limits for Unmarked Tiedowns.

Carriers are advised to purchase and use components that are rated and marked by their manufacturer. That way, the carrier, driver, shipper, and inspector can all verify that the proper equipment is being used for the job.

In Canada, unmarked tiedowns (or their components) are prohibited effective January 1, 2010.

U.S. rules do not currently require that anchor points be rated or marked, and they do not prohibit the use of unmarked tiedown devices.

2.3 Containing, Immobilizing, and Securing Cargo

Note the following specific requirements for **unmarked** tiedowns:

TYPE	REQUIREMENT
Synthetic cordage (e.g., nylon, polypropylene, polyester) which is unmarked as to composition or WLL	WLL is equal to that for polypropylene fiber rope
Welded steel chain which is unmarked as to grade or WLL	WLL is equal to that for grade 30 proof coil chain
Unmarked wire rope	WLL is equal to one-fourth of the nominal strength listed in the Wire Rope Users Manual
Wire which is unmarked as to construction type	WLL is equal to that for 6x37 fiber core wire rope
Unmarked manila rope	WLL is based on its diameter as provided in the WLL tables
Unmarked friction mats	Assumed to provide resistance to horizontal movement equal to 50% of the weight placed on the mat

Working load limits: marked components

Some manufacturers mark their securement devices with a **numeric WLL value**. The WLL for these devices is equal to the numeric value assigned by the manufacturer.

Other manufacturers mark components using a **code or symbol** that is defined in a recognized standard. For example: A piece of grade 7 chain may be marked with a 70 or 700, in accordance with the standard of the National Association of Chain Manufacturers. The standard then gives the WLL for that piece of chain, depending on its size.

Tiedown materials marked by the manufacturer with working load limits that differ from the tables shown in chapter 4.6 are considered to have a WLL equal to the value for which they are marked.

Chain grades are generally marked with raised numbers and/or letters, and the marking spacing varies from every link to every 3 feet. If the marking is worn or rusty and difficult to read, use a wire brush to clean the link and a light to read the marking.

2.3 Containing, Immobilizing, and Securing Cargo

Aggregate working load limit

The sum of the working load limits of each device used to secure an article on a vehicle is called the aggregate working load limit. Knowing the aggregate WLL will allow you to determine the minimum number of tiedowns required for your cargo, based on the weight of the cargo.

How do you calculate the aggregate WLL?

To calculate the aggregate WLL, add together:

- 50% of the WLL of each direct tiedown (tiedowns that go from an anchor point on the vehicle to an attachment point on an article of cargo, or which pass through, over, or around the cargo and are then attached to an anchor point on the same side of the vehicle); AND

- 100% of the WLL of each indirect tiedown (tiedowns that go from an anchor point on the vehicle, through, over, or around the cargo and then attach to another anchor point on the other side of the vehicle).

Examples:

50% of A
+ 50% of B
+ 50% of C
+ 50% of D
= Aggregate WLL

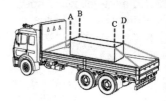

100% of A
+ 100% of B
= Aggregate WLL

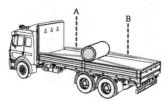

100% of A
+ 100% of B
= Aggregate WLL

2.3 Containing, Immobilizing, and Securing Cargo

Canada does not differentiate between the contributions of direct and indirect tiedowns to the aggregate WLL. Rather, the aggregate WLL is defined to be the sum of 50% of the WLL for each end section of a tiedown that is attached to an anchor point on the vehicle or cargo.

What should the aggregate WLL be?

The aggregate working load limit of any securement system must be **at least 50% of the weight of the cargo** being secured. If it's less, you need to add more straps or securement components.

For example, suppose you have load straps with a WLL of 5,000 pounds (2,268 kg) and you are securing 40,000 pounds (18,144 kg) of cargo on a flatbed using an indirect tiedown method. How many tiedowns would you need?

First, you know that the aggregate WLL of the securement system must be at least 20,000 pounds (9,072 kg), or 50% of the weight of the cargo. Because you are using an indirect tiedown method, you can use 100% of the WLL of each strap.

Therefore, four tiedowns are needed:

$$20,000 \div 5,000 = 4$$

When the aggregate WLL does not divide evenly into 50% of the cargo weight, always round up the result. For example, if the cargo in our example weighed 20,100 pounds, five tiedowns would be needed.

$$20,100 \div 5,000 = 4.02 \text{ (round up to 5)}$$

If we used a direct tiedown method in the above example, we would need 8 tiedowns, because when determining the aggregate WLL, we can only count 50% of the WLL of each tiedown, so:

$$20,000 \div 2,500 = 8$$

2.3 Containing, Immobilizing, and Securing Cargo

Putting it all together

Recall that the number of tiedowns and securement devices needed depends on whether the cargo is prevented from moving forward, the length and weight of the cargo, and the strength of the tiedown. You need to consider all three factors when deciding how best to secure a load.

For example, suppose your cargo is 16 feet (4.9 m) long and weighs 45,000 pounds (20,412 kg). You are not placing the cargo against a bulkhead or other cargo, your tiedown straps have a WLL of 4,000 pounds (1,814 kg), and you are using an indirect tiedown method. How many straps do you need?

Based on the placement and length of the cargo, you need at least 3 tiedowns (the cargo is more than 10 feet long but less than 20, and forward movement is not prevented). However, the straps are not strong enough to hold the cargo if you use only 3, based on the WLL of the straps:

$$22,500 \div 4,000 = 5.63$$

Therefore, you need to use **at least 6 straps**.

What if, instead of straps, you use Grade 70 chain with a WLL of 11,300 pounds? Based on the aggregate WLL of the chains, it would seem that you need only 2:

$$22,500 \div 11,300 = 1.99$$

But because the cargo is 16 feet long, you must use at least 3 chains for this load.

2.4 Inspection Requirements

The driver is responsible for the following cargo securement inspection activities.

Action	Pre-trip	Within first 50 miles (80 km)	When duty status changes	Every 3 hours or 150 miles (240 km), whichever is first
Inspect cargo and securing devices	✔	✔	✔	✔
Inform carrier if packaging is not adequate	✔			
Adjust cargo and/or securing devices	As necessary	As necessary	As necessary	As necessary
Add additional securing devices	As necessary	As necessary	As necessary	As necessary

2.4 Inspection Requirements

Driver securement inspection checklist

<u>Pre-trip</u>

- Make sure that cargo is properly distributed and adequately secured (according to the regulations).
- Make sure that all securement equipment and vehicle structures are in good working order and used consistent with their capability.
- Stow vehicle equipment.
- Make sure that nothing obscures front and side views or interferes with the ability to drive the vehicle or respond in an emergency.

> The inspection rules do not apply to the driver of a sealed commercial motor vehicle who has been ordered not to open it to inspect its cargo or to the driver of a commercial motor vehicle that has been loaded in a manner that makes inspection of its cargo impracticable.

- Inform carrier if packaging is not adequate. For example:
  - Banding is loose or not symmetrical on package.
  - Banding attachment device(s) are inefficient.
  - Wrapping is broken or ineffective.
  - Pallets are broken.

<u>Periodic inspections during transit</u>

- Inspect cargo and securing devices.
- Adjust cargo or load securement devices as necessary to ensure that cargo cannot shift on or within, or fall from, the commercial motor vehicle.
- As necessary, add more securing devices.

3. COMMODITY-SPECIFIC SECUREMENT REQUIREMENTS
3.1 Logs

Shortwood	40
Longwood	40
Vehicle requirements	41
Stakes	41
Log packing requirements	42
General tiedown requirements	42
Log securement requirements	43
Common vehicle types	44
Shortwood loaded crosswise on frame, rail, and flatbed vehicles	44
Securing logs loaded lengthwise on flatbed and frame vehicles	47
Logs transported on pole trailers	48

The regulations specify securement practices for a variety of specific commodities, beginning with logs.

Included in this category is all natural wood that retains the original shape of the bole (trunk) of a tree whether raw, partially processed, or fully processed.

3.1 Logs

- Raw — All tree species that have been harvested, with bark; may have been trimmed or cut to length.
- Partially processed — Fully or partially debarked, or further reduced in length.
- Fully processed — Utility poles, treated poles, log cabin building components.

The specific requirements for logs cover shortwood and longwood.

Shortwood

- Normally up to about 100 inches (2.5 m) in length.
- No longer than 16 feet (4.9 m) in length.
- Also called:
  - Cut-up logs
  - Cut-to-length logs
  - Bolts
  - Pulpwood

Longwood

- Anything not considered shortwood.
- Includes utility poles.
- Also called:
  - Long logs
  - Treelength

The following types of logs are NOT covered by the log-specific requirements:

- Logs unitized by banding or other comparable means. These must be secured according to the general cargo securement requirements.
- Loads of no more than four processed logs. These also must be secured according to the general cargo securement requirements.
- Firewood, stumps, debris, other short logs, and longer logs. Transport these in a vehicle or container that is enclosed on four sides (front, back, left, right) and strong enough to contain them.

3.1 Logs

> Some stacks may be made up of both shortwood and longwood. Any stack that includes shortwood must follow the shortwood securement requirements, except that if shortwood is embedded in a load of longwood, it can be treated as longwood.

Vehicle requirements

Vehicles used to transport logs must be designed and built, or adapted, for transportation of logs.

- Vehicle must be fitted with a means to cradle the logs and prevent rolling, such as:
  - Bunks
  - Bolsters
  - Stakes
  - Standards
- All vehicle components must be designed and built to withstand all anticipated operational forces without failure, accidental release, or permanent deformation.

Stakes

If stakes or standards are not permanently attached to the vehicle, secure the stakes so that they do not separate from the vehicle.

3.1 Logs

Log packing requirements

- Logs must be solidly packed.
- Outer bottom logs must be in contact with and rest solidly against bunks, bolsters, stakes, or standards.
- Each outside log on the side of a stack of logs must touch at least two bunks, bolsters, stakes, or standards. If one end of the log doesn't touch a stake:
  - It must rest on other logs in a stable manner.
  - It must extend beyond the stake, bunk, bolster, or standard.
- The center of the highest log on each side or end must be below the top of each stake, bunk, or standard.

 In Canada, the upper logs that form the top of the load must be crowned.

General tiedown requirements

Tiedowns must be used in combination with the bunks, stakes, and bolsters to secure the load UNLESS the logs:

- Are transported in a crib-type log trailer, and
- Are loaded in compliance with the requirements shown on pages 41-43.

3.1 Logs

Use tiedowns to secure logs that are not held in place by contact with other logs or the stakes, bunks, or standards.

The aggregate working load limit for tiedowns used to secure a stack of logs on a frame vehicle, or a flatbed vehicle equipped with bunks, bolsters, or stakes, must be at least one-sixth the weight of the stack of logs.

In Canada:
- Tiedowns must be used with crib-type log trailers (Canada has not adopted the U.S. definition of "crib-type log trailer").
- For logs loaded lengthwise, the aggregate WLL of tiedowns used to secure each stack must be at least $1/6^{th}$ of the weight of the stack. For shortwood, the tiedown aggregate WLL must be 1/2 of the stack weight.

Log securement requirements

- Tighten tiedowns at initial loading.
    - Do not tension beyond the tiedown's working load limit.
- Check the load and tiedowns again when you get to a public road, in addition to the intervals specified in chapter 2.4. Adjust the load and tiedowns as needed.
- Use additional tiedowns or securing devices when there is low friction between logs and they are likely to slip on each other (for example, when logs are wet).

3.1 Logs

Common vehicle types

Rail Vehicle

Frame Vehicle

Flatbed Vehicle

Shortwood loaded crosswise on frame, rail, and flatbed vehicles

Logs loaded crosswise on these vehicles must meet the following requirements in addition to the previously described packing and securement requirements.

Lower tier requirements

- The end of a log in the lower tier must never extend more than 1/3 of the log's total length beyond the nearest supporting structure. This prevents tipping when the vehicle turns.

Tiedown requirements

- Use two tiedowns to secure one stack of shortwood loaded crosswise.
    - Attach the tiedowns to the vehicle frame at the front and rear of the load.
- Position tiedowns at approximately 1/3 and 2/3 of the length of the logs.

3.1 Logs

 After Jan. 1, 2010, new vehicles must be equipped with a device that maintains a tension of not less than 900 kg at all times, and automatically takes up slack in the tiedown as the logs settle.

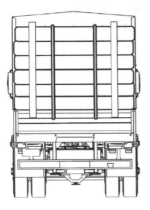

Requirements for vehicles over 33 feet (10 m)

Vehicles over 33 feet (10 m) long must be equipped with center stakes, or comparable devices, to divide it into sections of equal length.

- Each tiedown must:
    - Secure the highest log on each side of the center stake.
    - Be fastened below these logs.
- Three securement options:

    Option #1:
    - Tiedowns may be fixed at each end and tensioned from the middle.

    Option #2:
    - Tiedowns may be fixed in the middle and tensioned from each end.

3.1 Logs

Option #3:

- Tiedowns may pass through a pulley or equivalent device in the middle and be tensioned from one end.

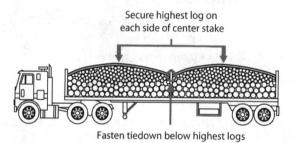

Secure highest log on each side of center stake

Fasten tiedown below highest logs

Stakes/structure and tiedown requirements

Anchor any structure or stake that is being forced upward when the tiedowns are being tensioned, to resist that force.

Additional securement requirements for two stacks side-by-side

- In addition to the requirements for shortwood loaded crosswise, load two stacks side-by-side so that:

    - There is no space between the two stacks of logs.

    - The outside of each stack is raised at least 1 inch (2.5 cm) within 4 inches (10 cm) of the end of the logs or from the side of the vehicle.

    - The highest log is no more than 8 feet (2.44 m) above the deck.

    - At least one tiedown is used lengthwise across each stack.

3.1 Logs

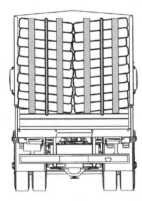

Acceptable securement of two stacks of shortwood logs loaded crosswise. Note how the logs slope inward.

Securing logs loaded lengthwise on flatbed and frame vehicles

Shortwood loaded lengthwise

- Meet the packing and securement requirements as previously described.
- Cradle each stack in a bunk unit or contain each stack with stakes.

Choose one of 3 options:

1. Secure each stack to the vehicle with at least two tiedowns; OR

2. Secure each stack to the vehicle with one tiedown (positioned about midway between the stakes) IF all the logs in each stack are:

    - Blocked in the front by a front-end structure strong enough to restrain the load, or by another stack of logs, and

    - Blocked in the rear by another stack of logs or vehicle end structure; OR

3. Bind each stack with at least two tiedown-type devices such as wire rope, used as wrappers that encircle the entire load at locations along the load that provide effective securement (Note: The wrappers do not have to be attached to the vehicle).

 In Canada, to use option #2 above, the logs must be shorter than 3.04 meters (10 ft). Option #3 (using unattached wrappers) is only allowed on pole trailers.

3.1 Logs

Longwood loaded lengthwise

- Cradle the logs in two or more bunks.

Either:

- Secure the logs to the vehicle by at least 2 tiedowns at locations that provide effective securement, OR
- Bind the logs with tiedown-type devices such as wire rope used as a wrapper that encircles the entire load at locations along the load that provide effective securement.
  - If a wrapper is being used to bundle the logs together, it does not have to be attached to the vehicle.

 In Canada, unattached wrappers are only allowed on pole trailers.

Logs transported on pole trailers

Secure the load in one of these ways:

- At least one tiedown at each bunk, OR
- At least two tiedowns used as wrappers that encircle the entire load.

Wrapper requirements

- Position front and rear wrappers at least 10 feet (3.04 m) apart.

Large logs

- Use chock blocks or similar means to prevent the shifting of large diameter single and double log loads.

Large diameter logs that are above the bunks must be secured to the underlying load with at least two additional wrappers.

48

3.2 Dressed Lumber and Similar Building Materials

Positioning and securing bundles 50
Bundles in one tier 51
Bundles in two or more tiers 52
Suggestion to increase safety 55

The requirements for dressed lumber and similar building materials apply to certain products when they are transported as bundles on flatbed and open vehicles.

These products are:

- Dressed lumber
- Packaged lumber
- Engineered building products (e.g. plywood, drywall, and other materials of similar shape)

"Bundle" refers to packages of lumber, building materials, or similar products which are unitized for securement as a single article of cargo.

 Lumber or building products that are not bundled or packaged should be treated as loose items and transported in accordance with the general cargo securement requirements.

3.2 Dressed Lumber and Similar Building Materials

 Bundles carried in a closed vehicle should be immobilized or contained in accordance with the general cargo securement requirements.

Positioning and securing bundles

Choose one of two options for positioning bundles placed side by side on a platform vehicle:

<u>Option #1</u>: Place bundles in direct contact with each other.

<u>Option #2</u>: Provide a means (such as dunnage or blocking) to prevent the bundles from shifting towards each other.

 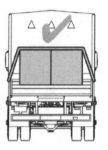

3.2 Dressed Lumber and Similar Building Materials

Bundles in one tier

- Secure bundles in accordance with general cargo securement requirements.
- Web tiedowns are often used to secure building materials.

Requirements for securement system:
- In proper working order with no damaged or weakened components that affect their performance or reduce their working load limit.
- No knots.
- Attached and secured in a manner that prevents them from coming loose during transit.
- Able to be tightened by a driver of an in-transit vehicle.
- Located inboard of rub rails whenever practicable.
- Edge protection must be used when a tiedown would be subject to abrasion or cutting.

3.2 Dressed Lumber and Similar Building Materials

Bundles in two or more tiers

There are five options for securing bundles of dressed lumber that are transported in two or more tiers. Choose one of the five.

Option #1: To block side-to-side movement, block the bundles with stakes on the sides of the vehicle. Secure the bundles by tiedowns laid out over the top tier, as outlined in the general cargo securement requirements.

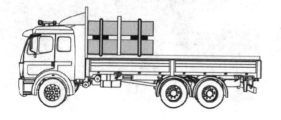

Option #2: To block side-to-side movement, use blocking or high-friction devices between the tiers. Secure the bundles by tiedowns laid out over the top tier, as outlined in the general cargo securement requirements.

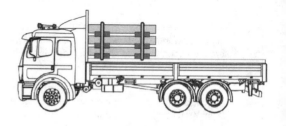

 High-friction devices include:
- Friction mats
- Pieces of wood with friction surface
- Cleated mats
- Other specialized equipment

3.2 Dressed Lumber and Similar Building Materials

Option #3: Place bundles directly on top of other bundles or on spacers. Secure the stack of bundles with tiedowns over the top tier of bundles, with a minimum of 2 tiedowns over each top bundle longer than 5 feet (1.52 m). In addition:

- If there are 3 tiers, secure the middle and top bundles with tiedowns in accordance with the general cargo securement requirements; OR

- If there are more than 3 tiers, secure one of the middle bundles and the top bundle with tiedown devices in accordance with the general cargo securement requirements. The maximum height for the middle tier that must be secured may not exceed 6 feet (1.83 m) above the deck of the trailer. Otherwise, secure the second tier from the bottom in accordance with the general cargo securement requirements.

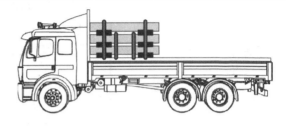

 Spacer requirements:
- The length of spacers must provide support to all pieces in the bottom row of the bundle.
- The width of each spacer must be equal or greater than the height.
- If spacers are comprised of layers of material, the layers must be unitized or fastened together to ensure that the spacer performs as a single piece of material.

3.2 Dressed Lumber and Similar Building Materials

Minimum tiedowns required for option #3

Stack length/weight	Layers/tiers in stack	Forward movement is NOT blocked — Tiedowns required over top layer in stack	Forward movement is NOT blocked — Tiedowns required over middle layer in stack	Forward movement is blocked — Tiedowns required over top layer in stack	Forward movement is blocked — Tiedowns required over middle layer in stack
5´ or less and 1,100 lbs. or less	2	1	None required	1	None required
	3	1	1	1	1
	over 3	1	1, not more than 6´ above deck	1	1, not more than 6´ above deck
5´ or less and over 1,100 lbs.	2	2	None required	1	None required
	3	2	2	1	1
	over 3	2	2, not more than 6´ above deck	1	1, not more than 6´ above deck
Over 5´ but 10´ or less	2	2	None required	2	None required
	3	2	2	2	1
	over 3	2	2, not more than 6´ above deck	2	1, not more than 6´ above deck
Longer than 10´	2	2 for first 10´, plus 1 for every additional 10´ or part thereof	None required	1 for every 10´ or part thereof	None required
	3	2 for first 10´, plus 1 for every additional 10´ or part thereof	2 for first 10´, plus 1 for every additional 10´ or part thereof	1 for every 10´ or part thereof	1 for every 10´ or part thereof
	over 3	2 for first 10´, plus 1 for every additional 10´ or part thereof	2 for first 10´, plus 1 for every additional 10´ or part thereof, not more than 6´ above deck	1 for every 10´ or part thereof	1 for every 10´ or part thereof, not more than 6´ above deck

Metric conversions: 5ft = 1.52m; 6ft = 1.83m; 10ft = 3.04m; 1,100lbs = 500kg. ***Remember:** Aggregate WLL must be 50% of cargo weight.

3.2 Dressed Lumber and Similar Building Materials

Option #4: Secure the bundles by tiedowns over each tier of bundles in accordance with the general cargo securement requirements.

- Use at least 2 tiedowns over each bundle on the top tier that is longer than 5 feet (1.52 m).

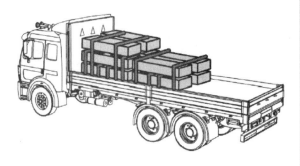

Option #5: Load the materials in a sided vehicle or container of adequate strength and secure them in accordance with the general cargo securement requirements.

Suggestion to increase safety

Choose one of two options for stopping forward motion:

1. Place bundles against bulkhead/front end structure.
2. When different tiers need to be secured, use a combination of blocking equipment and tiedowns.

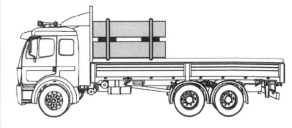

3.2 Dressed Lumber and Similar Building Materials

3.3 Metal Coils

Size of coil 57
Orientation of coil 58
Type of vehicle 58
Coils transported with eyes vertical on a vehicle with anchor points 59
Transporting coils with eyes crosswise on a vehicle with anchor points 61
Transporting coils with eyes lengthwise on a vehicle with anchor points 63
Transporting coil in a sided vehicle or intermodal container without anchor points . . 68

This section applies to articles of cargo comprised of elements, mixtures, compounds, or alloys commonly known as metal, metal foil, metal leaf, forged metal, stamped metal, metal wire, metal rod, or metal chain that are packaged as a roll, coil, spool, wind, or wrap, including plastic or rubber coated electrical wire and communications cable.

 Canada has not adopted the U.S. definition of "metal coil" and applies the rules more narrowly to coils of rolled sheet metal.

Size of coil

All metal coil shipments that, individually or together, weigh 5,000 pounds (2,268 kg) or more must be secured according to the specific requirements in this section. Coils that weigh less than 5,000 pounds (2,268 kg) may be secured according to the general securement requirements.

3.3 Metal Coils

Orientation of coil

There are generally three ways to orient coils on a vehicle, with specific securement requirements for each:

- Eyes vertical

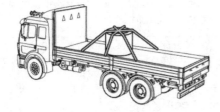

- Eyes crosswise

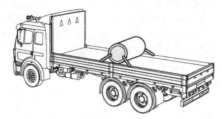

- Eyes lengthwise

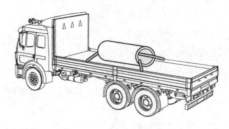

Type of vehicle

The securement rules are for metal coils transported:

- On flatbed vehicles.
- In sided vehicles with or without anchor points.
- In intermodal containers with or without anchor points.

3.3 Metal Coils

Coils transported with <u>eyes vertical</u> on a vehicle <u>with anchor points</u>

If the coil is mounted on a pallet:

- Coil must be fastened to pallet so it cannot move on the pallet.
- Pallet must be strong enough to not collapse under Performance Criteria forces.
- Use a friction mat between pallet and deck.

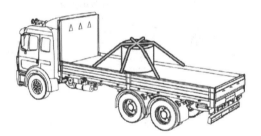

Requirements for securing a single coil

- To prevent the coil from tipping, arrange tiedowns to include the following:
    - Attach at least one tiedown diagonally across eye of coil from left side of vehicle to right side of vehicle.
    - Attach at least one tiedown diagonally across eye of coil from right side of vehicle to left side of vehicle.
    - Attach at least one tiedown over eye of coil from side-to-side.
    - To prevent forward movement, use one of these:
        o Blocking
        o Bracing
        o Friction mats
        o A tiedown passed around front of coil

3.3 Metal Coils

Requirements for securing a row of coils

When coils are grouped and loaded side by side in a transverse or longitudinal row, each row of coils must be secured by the following:

- Attach at least one tiedown against front of row of coils to restrain against forward motion.
  - If possible, the angle between tiedown and deck should be less than 45°, when viewed from the side of the vehicle.
- Attach at least one tiedown against rear of row of coils to restrain against rearward motion.
  - If possible, the angle between tiedown and deck should be less than 45°, when viewed from the side of the vehicle.
- Attach at least one tiedown over top of each coil or side-by-side row of coils to restrain against vertical motion.
  - Tiedowns going over top of coil(s) must be as close as possible to eye of coil.
- Arrange tiedowns, blocking, or bracing to prevent shifting or tipping in all directions.

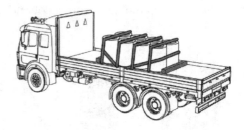

3.3 Metal Coils

Transporting coils with <u>eyes crosswise</u> on a vehicle <u>with anchor points</u>

There are three requirements for coils transported with eyes crosswise:

1. Prevent the coil from rolling.
2. Attach one tiedown forward.
3. Attach one tiedown rearward.

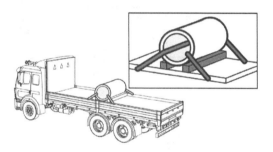

Requirements for securing a single coil

To prevent the coil from rolling:

- Support the coil.
    - Use timbers, chocks, or wedges held in place by coil bunks or similar devices to prevent them from coming loose.
    - Use a cradle (for example, two hardwood timbers and two coil bunks) that is restrained from sliding by:
        o Friction mats under the cradle.
        o Nailed wood blocking or cleats.
        o Placing a tiedown around the front of the cradle.
- The support must:
    - Support the coil just above the deck.
    - Not become unintentionally unfastened or loose in transit.

3.3 Metal Coils

 The use of nailed blocking or cleats as the sole means to secure timbers, chocks or wedges, or a nailed wood cradle, is prohibited.

Forward tiedown:

- Attach at least one tiedown through the eye of the coil to restrain against forward motion.
  - If possible, the angle between the tiedown and the deck should be less than 45°.

Rearward tiedown:

- Attach at least one tiedown through the eye of the coil to restrain against rearward motion.
  - If possible, the angle between the tiedown and the deck should be less than 45°.

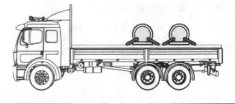

 If a tiedown is used around the front of the cradle, it does not count towards the aggregate WLL for tiedowns through the eye of the coil.

3.3 Metal Coils

 Attaching tiedowns diagonally through the eye of a coil to form an X-pattern when viewed from above the vehicle is prohibited when eyes are crosswise.

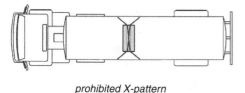

prohibited X-pattern

Transporting coils with <u>eyes lengthwise</u> on a vehicle <u>with anchor points</u>

Requirements for securing an individual coil

There are three options for safely securing individual coils that are loaded with their eyes lengthwise. Blocking and supporting the coils is the same. The difference is in the tiedown arrangement.

Prevent the coil from rolling by supporting it:

- Use timbers, chocks, or wedges held in place by coil bunks or similar devices to prevent them from coming loose.

- Use a cradle (for example, two hardwood timbers and two coil bunks) that is restrained from sliding by:

    - Placing friction mats under the cradle.

3.3 Metal Coils

- Using nailed wood blocking or cleats against the front timber.
- Placing a tiedown around the front of the cradle.

• The support must:
- Support the coil off the deck.
- Not become unintentionally unfastened or loose in transit.

 The use of nailed blocking or cleats as the sole means to secure timbers, chocks or wedges, or a nailed wood cradle, is prohibited

Use one of the following three options to secure the coil:

Option #1

• Attach at least one tiedown diagonally from the left side of the vehicle, through the eye, to the right side of the vehicle.
- If possible, the angle between the tiedown and the deck should be less than 45°, when viewed from the side of the vehicle.

• Attach at least one tiedown diagonally from the right side of the vehicle, through the eye, to the left side of the vehicle.
- If possible, the angle between the tiedown and the deck should be less than 45°, when viewed from the side of the vehicle.

• Attach at least one tiedown side-to-side over the top of the coil.

3.3 Metal Coils

- Use blocking or friction mats to prevent forward movement.

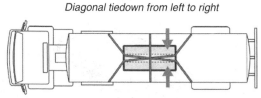

Diagonal tiedown from left to right

Diagonal tiedown from right to left

Option #2

Option #2 is the same as Option #1, except the tiedowns that attach through the eye of the coil are straight instead of diagonal.

- Attach at least one tiedown straight from the left side of the vehicle, through the eye, and back to the left side of the vehicle.
    - If possible, the angle between the tiedown and the deck should be less than 45°, when viewed from the side of the vehicle.

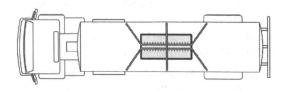

- Attach at least one tiedown straight from the right side of the vehicle, through the eye, and back to the right side of the vehicle.
    - If possible, the angle between the tiedown and the deck should be less than 45°, when viewed from the side of the vehicle.
- Attach at least one tiedown side-to-side over the top of the coil.
- Use blocking or friction mats to prevent forward movement.

3.3 Metal Coils

Option #3

Option #3 is the same as Options #1 and #2, except that the two tiedowns that attach through the eye of the coil are replaced with two tiedowns that pass over the front and the rear of the coil.

- Attach at least one tiedown over the top of the coil near the front of the coil.
- Attach at least one tiedown over the top of the coil near the rear of the coil.
- Use blocking or friction mats to prevent forward movement.

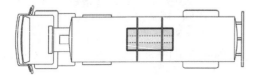

Requirements for securing rows of coils

A row of coils is three or more coils loaded in the same way and in a line.

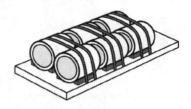

Prevent the coil from rolling by supporting it:

- Use timbers, chocks, or wedges held in place by coil bunks or similar devices to prevent them from coming loose.
- Use a cradle (for example, two hardwood timbers and two coil bunks) that is restrained from sliding by:
    - Placing friction mats under the cradle
    - Using nailed wood blocking or cleats against the front timber

3.3 Metal Coils

- Placing a tiedown around the front of the cradle.
- The support must:
  - Support the coil just above the deck.
  - Not become unintentionally unfastened or loose in transit.

The use of nailed blocking or cleats as the sole means to secure timbers, chocks or wedges, or a nailed wood cradle, is prohibited.

Attach tiedowns as follows:

- Attach at least one tiedown over the top of each coil or side-by-side row, located near the front of the coil.
- Attach at least one tiedown over the top of each coil or side-by-side row, located near the rear of the coil.
- Use blocking, bracing, or friction mats to prevent forward movement.

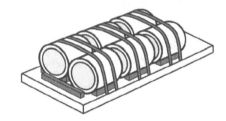

3.3 Metal Coils

Transporting coil in a sided vehicle or intermodal container <u>without anchor points</u>

To prevent metal coils from moving horizontally and/or tipping:

- Follow general cargo securement requirements
- Secure the coils using:
  - Blocking and bracing
  - Friction mats
  - A combination of these

The securement system used must prevent horizontal movement and tipping.

3.4 Paper Rolls

Loading and securing paper rolls with eyes
vertical in a sided vehicle 70

Loading and securing paper rolls with eyes
horizontal in a sided vehicle 76

Loading and securing paper rolls with eyes
lengthwise in a sided vehicle 79

Loading and securing paper rolls on a flatbed
vehicle or a curtain-sided vehicle 80

The rules in this section apply to shipments of paper rolls which, individually or together, weigh 5,000 pounds (2,268 kg) or more.

 Shipments of paper rolls that weigh less than 5,000 pounds (2,268 kg) and paper rolls that are unitized on a pallet may either be secured in accordance this chapter or with the general cargo securement requirements.

 This chapter does not apply to small rolls of paper shipped in cartons/containers such as toilet paper or paper towels that would be used in the kitchen. This type of product is covered in the general cargo securement requirements.

3.4 Paper Rolls

Plan your securement system for paper rolls.

- Select a good load pattern.
- Block, brace, or immobilize paper rolls to make sure they are prevented from sliding, tipping, or rolling.
- Prevent significant movement of small groups of paper rolls when movement is not prevented by other cargo or by the vehicle structure.
- Symmetrically stack paper rolls when eyes are horizontal.
- Make sure that stacks are secured to prevent significant movement.
- Use friction mats to prevent horizontal movement. Such mats can provide significant benefits in preventing slippage.
- Use tiedowns that pass over the paper rolls to increase the effect of friction.
- Use tiedowns when rolls are loaded on flatbeds or curtain-sided vehicles.

Loading and securing paper rolls with <u>eyes vertical</u> in a <u>sided vehicle</u>

Requirements for placement

- Place paper rolls together in a group so that the structure of the group can be maintained.
- Place paper rolls tightly against:
  - The front and walls of the vehicle
  - Each other
  - Other cargo
- Usually the roll is secure if a paper roll has 3 well-separated points of contact with the vehicle, other rolls, or other cargo.

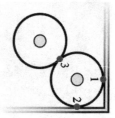

3 points of contact

3.4 Paper Rolls

Requirements for preventing side-to-side movement

If there are not enough paper rolls in the shipment to reach the walls of the vehicle, prevent side-to-side movement by one of these methods:

- Blocking
- Bracing
- Tiedowns
- Void fillers
- Friction mats
- Banding the rolls together

Requirements for preventing rearward movement

When any void behind a group of paper rolls (including rolls at the rear of the vehicle) is greater than the diameter of the paper rolls, prevent rearward movement by one of these methods:

- Friction mats
- Blocking
- Bracing
- Tiedowns
- Banding to other rolls

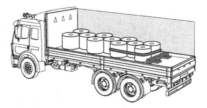

3.4 Paper Rolls

Requirements for preventing paper rolls from tipping

Situation #1:

- Paper roll is not prevented from tipping or falling sideways or rearwards by the vehicle structure or other cargo.
- Paper roll width is more than 2 times its diameter.

Solution #1:

Either:

- Band the roll to other rolls.
- Brace it.
- Use tiedowns.

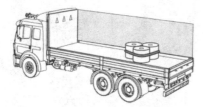

Situation #2:

- The forwardmost roll(s) in a group of paper rolls is not prevented from tipping or falling forward by vehicle structure or other cargo.
- Paper roll width is more than 1.75 times its diameter.

Solution #2:

Either:

- Band the roll to other rolls.
- Brace it.
- Use tiedowns.

3.4 Paper Rolls

Situation #3:

- A paper roll or the forwardmost roll(s) in a group of paper rolls is not prevented from tipping or falling forward by vehicle structure or other cargo.
- Paper roll width is more than 1.25 times its diameter.
- Blocking or other methods are used to prevent forward movement (friction mats are not used alone).

Solution #3:

The blocking tends to "trip" the roll so additional tipping securement is required.

Either:

- Band the roll to other rolls.
- Brace it.
- Use tiedowns.

Situation #4:

- The forwardmost roll(s) in a group of paper rolls has a width equal to or less than 1.75 times its diameter.
- Only friction mats are used for forward securement.

Solution #4:

The friction mat alone is adequate. The friction mat allows the roll to slide on the floor without tripping the roll.

3.4 Paper Rolls

Banding

If paper rolls are banded together:

- Place rolls tightly against each other to form a stable group.
- Apply bands tightly.
- Secure bands with tape, hangers, or other means so that the bands cannot fall off the rolls or slide down to the deck.

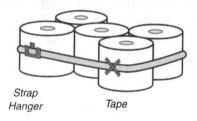

Strap Hanger   *Tape*

Requirements for friction mats

If a friction mat is used to provide the principal securement for a paper roll, insert the friction mat so that it sticks out from beneath the footprint of the roll in the direction in which it is providing securement (normally the front).

3.4 Paper Rolls

Requirements for split loads

Situation: A paper roll in a split load is not prevented from forward movement by the vehicle structure or other cargo.

Solution: Prevent forward movement by one of these methods.

- Friction mats
- Filling the open space
- Blocking
- Bracing
- Tiedowns
- Some combination of these

Requirements for stacked loads

- Load paper rolls on a second layer only if the bottom layer extends to the front of the vehicle.
- Prevent forward, rearward, or side-to-side movement by either:
  - Using the same means required for the bottom layer, OR
  - Using a blocking roll from a lower layer.
- A roll in the rearmost row of any layer raised using dunnage cannot be secured by friction mats alone.

 The blocking row must be at least 1.5 inches (38 mm) taller than other rolls, or must be raised at least 1.5 inches (38 mm) using dunnage.

 In Canada, a roll in the rearmost row of any layer must not be raised using dunnage.

3.4 Paper Rolls

Loading and securing paper rolls with <u>eyes horizontal</u> in a <u>sided vehicle</u>

Requirements for eyes crosswise: prevent forward and rearward movement

- To prevent paper rolls from rolling or shifting in the forward and rearward directions, either:
    - Position the rolls in contact with the vehicle structure or other cargo; OR
    - Use chocks, wedges, tiedowns, blocking, and bracing.

> Chocks, wedges, or blocking used to secure intermediate rolls from forward or rearward movement during loading do not have to be secured in place.

> Hold chocks, wedges, or blocking securing the front or rear roll in place by some means in addition to friction so they cannot become unintentionally unfastened or loose while the vehicle is in transit. This is often accomplished with nails.

3.4 Paper Rolls

Requirements for eyes crosswise: secure rearmost roll

Do <u>not</u> secure the rearmost roll with either:

- The rear doors of the vehicle or intermodal container, OR
- Blocking held in place by those doors.

The doors are not designed or intended as a cargo securing device. The rolls may push the doors open during transit or onto loading dock personnel when the doors are opened.

Requirements for eyes crosswise: prevent rolls from shifting toward either wall

If there is more than a total of 8 inches (203 mm) of space between the ends of a paper roll and other rolls or the walls of the vehicle, use one of these methods:

- Void fillers (such as honeycomb)
- Blocking
- Bracing
- Friction mats
- Tiedowns

3.4 Paper Rolls

Requirements for eyes crosswise: secure stacks of paper rolls from front-to-back movement

- Do not load paper rolls on a second layer unless the bottom layer extends to the front of the vehicle.

- Load paper rolls on higher layers only if all wells in the layer beneath are filled.

- Secure the foremost roll in each upper layer (or any roll with an empty well in front of it) against forward movement by either:

    - Placing it in a well formed by two rolls on the lower row whose diameter is equal to or greater than that of the roll on the upper row; OR

    - Banding it to other rolls; OR

    - Blocking it against an adequately secured, eye-vertical blocking roll resting on the floor of the vehicle that is at least 1.5 times taller than the diameter of the roll being blocked.

- If the rearmost roll in each upper layer is located in either of the last two wells formed by the rearmost rolls in the layer below, band it to the other rolls.

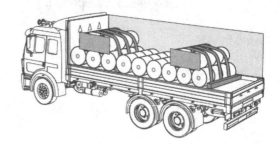

3.4 Paper Rolls

Requirements for eyes crosswise: prevent stacked rolls from shifting toward either wall

If there is more than a total of 8 inches (203 mm) of space between the ends of a paper roll and other rolls or the walls of the vehicle, use one of these methods.

- Void fillers (such as honeycomb)
- Blocking
- Bracing
- Friction mats
- Tiedowns

These are the same requirements that are used to secure a single layer of paper rolls.

Loading and securing paper rolls with <u>eyes lengthwise</u> in a <u>sided vehicle</u>

Requirements for eyes lengthwise: prevent movement

Potential Movement	Methods to Prevent Movement
Forward	- Vehicle structure - Other cargo - Blocking - Tiedowns
Rearward	- Other cargo - Blocking - Friction mats - Tiedowns
Side-to-side	- Vehicle wall - Other cargo - Chocks, wedges, or blocking of adequate size

3.4 Paper Rolls

 Hold chocks, wedges, or blocking in place by some means in addition to friction so they cannot become unintentionally unfastened or loose while the vehicle is in transit. This is often accomplished with nails.

Requirements for eyes lengthwise: stacked loads

- Do not load paper rolls in an upper layer if another roll will fit in the layer beneath.
- Form an upper layer by placing the paper rolls in the wells formed by the rolls beneath.
- Secure a roll in an upper layer against forward and rearward movement by either:
    - Using one of the means required for the bottom layer, OR
    - Using a blocking roll, OR
    - Banding it to other rolls.

Loading and securing paper rolls on a <u>flatbed vehicle</u> or a <u>curtain-sided vehicle</u>

Requirements for eyes vertical or with eyes horizontal and lengthwise

- Load and secure the paper rolls as described for a sided vehicle.
- Attach tiedowns to secure entire load according to the general cargo securement requirements.

 Stacked loads of paper rolls with eyes vertical are prohibited.

3.4 Paper Rolls

Requirements for eyes crosswise

- Prevent each roll from rolling or shifting forward and rearward by using:
    - Contact with the vehicle structure.
    - Contact with other cargo.
    - Chocks, wedges, blocking, or bracing of adequate size.
    - Tiedowns.
- Use side-to-side or front-to-back tiedowns to prevent side-to-side movement.

> Chocks, wedges, and blocking must be held in place by some additional means to friction so they may not become unfastened or loose while the vehicle is in transit.

3.4 Paper Rolls

3.5 Concrete Pipe

What is exempt from these specific requirements?	83
Securing concrete pipe	84
General tiedown requirements	84
Blocking requirements	85
Arranging the load	86
Securing small pipe	89
Securing large pipe	92

The securement requirements specific to concrete pipe apply to the transportation of concrete pipe on platform/flatbed trailers or vehicles, and lowboy trailers.

What is exempt from these specific requirements?

Follow general cargo securement requirements when transporting the following pipe:

- Concrete pipe that is grouped together into a single rigid article that has no tendency to roll.

- Concrete pipe loaded in a sided vehicle or container.

- Concrete pipe with eyes vertical or loaded lengthwise.

 The Canadian standard specifically applies to concrete pipe loaded crosswise (transversely). Follow the general cargo securement requirements for concrete pipe with eyes vertical or loaded lengthwise.

3.5 Concrete Pipe

Securing concrete pipe

To make sure that concrete pipe does not roll or slide:

- Load pipe as compactly as possible.
- Immobilize symmetrically stacked pipes by securing them in groups.
- Use blocking systems and tiedowns to increase the effect of friction.

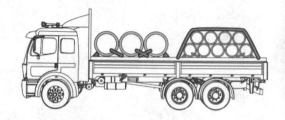

General tiedown requirements

- The aggregate working load limit of all tiedowns on any group of pipe must be at least 50% of the total weight of all pipes in the group.
- If you run a properly tensioned tiedown through a pipe in an upper tier or over lengthwise tiedowns, it will secure all the pipe beneath it on which the tiedown causes pressure.

3.5 Concrete Pipe

Blocking requirements

- Blocking must prevent the pipe from rolling or rotating.
- Blocking may be one or more pieces placed at equal distances from the center of a pipe.
    - When one piece of blocking is used, place it so that it extends at least half the distance from the center to each end of the pipe.
    - When two pieces of blocking are used, place them at each end of the pipe.

Blocking Option #2

Blocking Option #1

- Blocking must be:
    - Placed against the pipe, AND
    - Secured to prevent it from moving out from under the pipe.
- Timber blocking must have a minimum nominal dimension of 4 x 6 inches (8.9 x 14 cm).

3.5 Concrete Pipe

Arranging the load

Arranging pipe with different diameters

- Load pipe of more than one diameter in groups that consist of pipe of only one size.
- Secure each group of pipe separately.

Pipe with different diameters

Arranging a bottom tier

There are two ways to arrange the bottom tier:

- Cover the full length of the vehicle, OR

Bottom tier — Option #1

- Arrange as a partial tier in one or two groups.

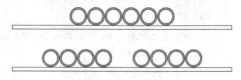

Bottom tier — Option #2

Arranging an upper tier

- Place pipe only in the wells formed by pipes in the tier below.
- Do not start an additional tier unless all wells in the tier beneath are filled.

3.5 Concrete Pipe

Arranging the top tier

- Arrange the top tier as a complete tier, a partial tier in one group, or a partial tier in two groups.

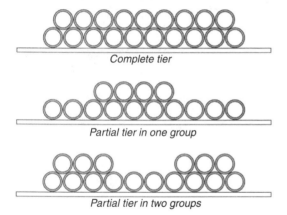

Complete tier

Partial tier in one group

Partial tier in two groups

Arranging bell pipe

- Load bell pipe on at least two longitudinal spacers tall enough to ensure that the bell is clear of the deck.

- If using <u>one tier</u>:

    - Load bell pipe so that the bells alternate on opposite sides of the vehicle.

    - If possible, the ends of consecutive pipe must be staggered within the allowable width.

    - If the ends cannot be staggered, they must be aligned.

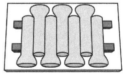 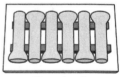

Staggered ends   *Aligned ends*

3.5 Concrete Pipe

- If using more than one tier:
  - Bells of the bottom tier must all be on the same side of the vehicle.
  - Bells of the upper tiers must be on the opposite side of the vehicle from the bells of the tier below.

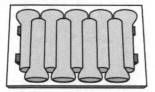

- If using more than one tier with a partial upper tier:
  - Pipes in the bottom tier that do not support a pipe above must have their bells alternating on opposite sides of the vehicle.

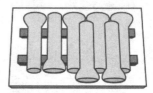

3.5 Concrete Pipe

Securing small pipe

Concrete pipe with an inside diameter up to 45 inches (114.3 cm) can form a complete single tier on a typical flatbed vehicle. Larger pipe often can only be carried as a partial tier.

> This pipe diameter of 45 in. (114.3 cm) is simply a convenient breaking point between "medium" and "large" diameter pipe.

Stabilizing the bottom tier

- Arrange the load properly
- Immobilize the front and rear pipe with one of the following elements:
  - Blocking
  - Wedges
  - Vehicle end structure
  - Stakes
  - Locked pipe unloader
  - Other equivalent means

- Hold other pipes in the bottom tier in place using blocks and/or wedges, if desired.
- Run tiedowns through the front and rear pipes to hold every pipe in the bottom tier firmly in contact with adjacent pipes:
  - The front tiedown must run rearward at an angle not more than 45° with the horizontal when viewed from the side of the vehicle, whenever practical.
  - The rear tiedown must run forward at an angle not more than 45° with the horizontal when viewed from the side of the vehicle, whenever practical.

3.5 Concrete Pipe

Tiedown requirements

Pipe may be secured individually or as a group:

<u>Individually</u>

- Run a chain though the pipe.

<u>As a group</u>

- Place a lengthwise tiedown(s) over the group of pipes, using either:
    - One 1/2 inch (1.27 cm) diameter chain or wire rope, OR
    - Two 3/8 inch (0.95 cm) diameter chains or wire ropes.
- Place one crosswise tiedown for every 10 feet (3.04 m) of load length. Either:
    - Attach the side-to-side tiedown through a pipe, OR
    - Pass the tiedown over both front-to-back tiedowns, between two pipes on the top tier.

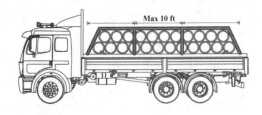

Stabilizing the top tier

If the <u>first pipe</u> of a group in the top tier is not placed in the first well formed by pipes at the front of the tier beneath:

- Secure it by attaching an additional tiedown that runs rearward at an angle not more than 45° to the horizontal when viewed from the side of the vehicle, whenever practicable.
- Pass the tiedown either through the front pipe of the upper tier or outside the front pipe and over both longitudinal tiedowns.

3.5 Concrete Pipe

If the <u>last pipe</u> of a group in the top tier is not placed in the last well formed by pipes at the rear of the tier beneath:

- Secure it by attaching an additional tiedown that runs forward at an angle not more than 45° to the horizontal when viewed from the side of the vehicle, whenever practicable.
- Pass the tiedown either through the rear pipe of the upper tier or outside the rear pipe and over both longitudinal tiedowns.

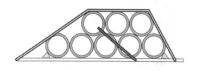

3.5 Concrete Pipe

Securing large pipe

"Large pipe" is concrete pipe with an inside diameter over 45 inches (114.3 cm).

Stabilizing the pipe

- Arrange the load properly
- Immobilize the front and rear pipe with one of the following methods:
    - Blocking
    - Wedges
    - Vehicle end structure
    - Stakes
    - Locked pipe unloader
    - Other equivalent means
- **For all other pipe, use additional blocks and/or wedges that are nailed in place.**

Securing the pipe

- Secure each pipe with tiedowns through the pipe.
- Run at least one tiedown through each pipe in the <u>front half</u> of the load. This includes the middle one if there is an odd number. The tiedown must run rearward at an angle not more than 45° with the horizontal when viewed from the side of the vehicle, whenever practicable.
- Run at least one tiedown through each pipe in the <u>rear half</u> of the load. The tiedown must run forward at an angle not more than 45° with the horizontal when viewed from the side of the vehicle, whenever practicable. This holds each pipe firmly in contact with adjacent pipe.

3.5 Concrete Pipe

- Run at least <u>two tiedowns</u> through the front and rear pipes (positioned as discussed above) if those pipes are **not** also in contact with the vehicle end structure, stakes, a locked pipe unloader, or other equivalent means.

 If only one pipe is transported, or if several pipes are transported without contact between other pipes, the requirements of this chapter apply to each pipe as a single front and rear article. Tiedowns must be used through that pipe.

3.5 Concrete Pipe

3.6 Intermodal Containers

Securing loaded intermodal containers on
container chassis vehicles 96

Securing loaded intermodal containers on
non-chassis vehicles 97

Securing empty intermodal containers on
non-chassis vehicles 98

The requirements in this chapter apply to the transportation of all intermodal containers.

 When securing cargo contained within an intermodal container, follow the general cargo securement requirements or, if applicable, follow the commodity-specific requirements.

3.6 Intermodal Containers

Securing <u>loaded</u> intermodal containers on <u>container chassis</u> vehicles

- Secure each intermodal container to the container chassis with securement or integral locking devices that cannot accidentally become unfastened. Integral locking devices do not have to be adjustable.

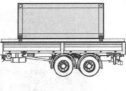

 If necessary, use secondary attachments to ensure that latches remain fastened in transit.

 Canadian standards specify that integral locking devices must be used.

- Secure <u>all lower corners</u> of the container to the container chassis.
- Securing devices must restrain the container from moving more than:
  - 1/2 inch (1.27 cm) forward, rearward, to the right, or to the left.
  - 1 inch (2.54 cm) vertically.
- Secure the front and rear of the container independently. Two latches on the chassis engage anchor points towards or at the front and rear of the container.
- If a latch is missing or broken, secure the corner by an alternative means, such as chain or wire rope.

3.6 Intermodal Containers

Securing <u>loaded</u> intermodal containers on <u>non-chassis</u> vehicles

- Position the intermodal container so that either:
  - All lower corners rest upon the vehicle; OR
  - The corners are supported by a structure capable of bearing the weight of the container. Independently secure the support structure to the vehicle.

- Secure each container to the vehicle by using either:
  - Chains, wire ropes, or integral devices that are fixed to all lower corners;
  - Crossed chains that are fixed to all upper corners; OR
  - Both of these methods.
- Secure the front and rear of the loaded container independently.
- The tiedowns must have an aggregate working load limit of at least 50% of the loaded weight of the loaded container.
- Attach each chain, wire rope, or integral locking device to the container in a manner that prevents it from becoming unfastened while in transit.

3.6 Intermodal Containers

Securing empty intermodal containers on non-chassis vehicles

Empty intermodal containers transported on non-chassis vehicles do not have to have all lower corners resting upon the vehicle or supported by a structure if they meet each of the following four requirements:

- Requirement 1: The container is balanced and positioned on the vehicle so it is stable before adding tiedowns or other securing devices.

- Requirement 2: The container does not hang over the front or rear of the trailer by more than 5 feet (1.5 m).

- Requirement 3: The container does not interfere with the vehicle's maneuverability.

- Requirement 4: The container is secured to prevent side-to-side, forward, rearward, and upward movement. Use either the requirements for loaded containers or follow the general cargo securement requirements.

3.7 Automobiles, Light Trucks, and Vans

Requirements for tiedowns designed
   to be affixed to the structure 100

Requirements for tiedowns designed
   to fit over or around the wheels 100

The requirements in this chapter apply to the transportation of automobiles, light trucks, and vans that individually weigh 10,000 pounds (4,500 kg) or less.

 Vehicles that are heavier than 10,000 pounds (4,500 kg) must be secured in accordance with the provisions of chapter 3.8, *Heavy Vehicles, Equipment, and Machinery.*

3.7 Automobiles, Light Trucks, and Vans

Tiedowns attached to the vehicle being transported are the most effective securement system.

- Use at least two tiedowns at both the front and rear of the cargo to prevent it from moving:
    - Side-to-side
    - Forward
    - Rearward
    - Vertically

 More tiedowns may be required to satisfy the general cargo securement requirement that the sum of the working load limits from all tiedowns must be at least 50% of the weight of the cargo.

Refer to page 107 for guidance on securing accessory equipment.

Requirements for tiedowns designed to be affixed to the structure

- These tiedowns must use the securement mounting points on the vehicle that have been designed for that purpose.

Requirements for tiedowns designed to fit over or around the wheels

- Provide restraint in the side-to-side, forward, rearward, and vertical directions.

Edge protectors are not required for synthetic webbing at points where the webbing comes in contact with the tires.

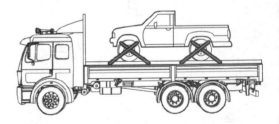

3.8 Heavy Vehicles, Equipment, and Machinery

Rules and industry best practices 102
Before loading: 102
During loading: 103
After loading: 103
Securement considerations 104
Minimum tiedown requirements 105
U.S. DOT guidance 107

The requirements in this chapter apply to the transportation of heavy vehicles, equipment, and machinery that:

- Operate on wheels or tracks, such as front end loaders, bulldozers, tractors, and power shovels.

- Individually weigh 10,000 pounds (4,500 kg) or more.

Other types of heavy industrial machinery such as generators, presses, transformers, etc., must be secured according to the general cargo securement requirements.

3.8 Heavy Vehicles, Equipment, and Machinery

Articles that are lighter than 10,000 pounds (4,500 kg) may be secured in accordance with:
- The provisions of this chapter; OR
- The general cargo securement requirements; OR
- Chapter 3.7, *Automobiles, Light Trucks, and Vans*.

Refer to the U.S. DOT guidance at the end of this chapter for more information.

Rules and industry best practices

The following is a combination of the regulatory requirements and industry best practices for the loading and securement of heavy equipment, vehicles, and machinery. When in doubt, be sure to comply at a minimum with the regulations found in §393.120 or the Canadian securement standards (see chapter 4.3).

Before loading:

- Determine the weight of the cargo and verify that the transport vehicle's gross vehicle weight rating (GVWR) and gross combination weight rating (GCWR) will not be exceeded.

- Determine your route and obtain any necessary permits for oversize/overwidth movements, if necessary.

- Determine if there are any specific loading guidelines that must be followed for the equipment, such as the use of locking pins, brakes, a certain transmission gear, or outriggers, deck wideners, etc.

- Determine where the equipment will be placed on the transport vehicle, paying particular attention to weight distribution and the ability to secure the equipment properly.

- Assess the equipment's securement points (if any) for wear and damage.

- If there will be low friction between the equipment and the transport vehicle (such as metal crawler

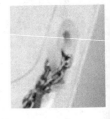

3.8 Heavy Vehicles, Equipment, and Machinery

tracks on a metal deck), determine if friction devices are necessary.

- Check the tire pressure on equipment with rubber tires — low or leaking tires may result in the loosening of tiedowns.

- Remove any excessive aggregate, dirt, debris, or other substances that may fall or reduce friction during transit.

During loading:

- Do not operate and/or load equipment or vehicles which you do not know how to operate properly or safely.

- To help prevent forward movement, place the equipment against a vehicle structure when possible, unless weight distribution or securement considerations require otherwise.

After loading:

- Completely lower all accessory equipment and other movable parts such as hydraulic shovels, booms, plows, crane arms, etc., and secure them to the transport vehicle using tiedowns. Accessories equipped with locking pins or similar devices which prevent movement in any direction do not have to be secured with additional securement devices. Hydraulics alone are not enough to secure accessory equipment.

103

3.8 Heavy Vehicles, Equipment, and Machinery

- Relieve any remaining hydraulic pressure on the equipment.
- Set the equipment's parking brake and steering lock.

- If the vehicle or equipment being transported has an articulation point (a permanent or semi-permanent pivot or hinge within its construction), lock or restrain the vehicle or equipment to prevent articulation while in transit.

- Accessories and other items that are not attached to the equipment must be secured to the transport vehicle following the general rules for cargo securement.
- Confirm the height and width of the vehicle after loading.

Securement considerations

- Be cautious when attaching securement devices over brake or hydraulic hoses, cylinders, etc., to avoid damaging those components.
- Use edge protection when necessary to prevent damage to tiedowns and/or the equipment.

3.8 Heavy Vehicles, Equipment, and Machinery

- Use the equipment manufacturer's designated attachment points when possible, and follow the manufacturer's securement recommendations.

- Do not use an attachment point if you are unsure of its strength or suitability.

- Though the regulations do not specify that chain must be used, chain is the preferred tiedown type for heavy equipment and machinery due to its strength and durability.

- Consider using direct tiedowns whenever possible (see chapter 2.3). Indirect tiedowns may be useful for accessory equipment and to prevent vertical movement ("bounce"). Direct tiedowns near each wheel (in addition to those required for securement) may also help reduce bounce.

- Prevent rolling of wheeled vehicles by using chocks, cradles, wedges, or other means placed against the wheels. Secure these securement devices to the vehicle.

Minimum tiedown requirements

- If the cargo has crawler tracks or wheels, you must use at least **four tiedowns** to prevent movement in the side-to-side, forward, rearward, and vertical directions.

- A single indirect tiedown routed through an anchor point and attached to both sides of the trailer is counted as a single tiedown.

3.8 Heavy Vehicles, Equipment, and Machinery

- In all cases, the sum of the working load limits of the tiedowns must equal at least 50% of the weight of the cargo. If you are unsure of the cargo's weight, additional tiedowns may be needed. Any tiedowns used to secure accessory equipment must not be included in this calculation.
- Attach tiedowns either:
    - As close as possible to the front and rear of the equipment, OR
    - At the mounting points on the equipment designed for that purpose.

In Canada, tiedowns for vehicles, equipment, or machinery with crawler tracks or wheels must each have a WLL of at least 2,268 kg (5,000 lb.).

More tiedowns may be required to satisfy the general cargo securement requirement that the sum of the working load limits from all tiedowns must be at least 50% of the weight of the cargo.

FOR EXAMPLE:

If you are securing a 35,000-pound loader with four direct chains, the combined WLL of the chains must be at least 17,500 pounds:

35,000# x 50% (or 0.5) = 17,500#

17,500# ÷ 4 chains = 4,375# WLL each

Recall that when using direct tiedowns, you can count only half the WLL of each tiedown (see chapter 2.3). Therefore, each chain must have a WLL of at least 8,750 pounds:

4,375 x 2 = 8,750# WLL each

In this case, four 7/16" Grade 70 transport chains (WLL = 8,750#) may suffice.

3.8 Heavy Vehicles, Equipment, and Machinery

U.S. DOT guidance

Question: If an item of construction equipment which weighs less than 10,000 pounds is transported on a flatbed or drop-deck trailer, must the accessory equipment be lowered to the deck of the trailer?

Guidance: No. However, the accessory equipment must be properly secured using locking pins or similar devices in order to prevent either the accessory equipment or the item of construction equipment itself from shifting during transport.

Question: How should I secure the accessories for an item of construction equipment which weighs 10,000 pounds or more, if the accessory devices would extend beyond the width of the trailer if they are lowered to the deck for transport?

Guidance: The accessory devices (plows, trencher bars, and the like) may be transported in a raised position, provided they are designed to be transported in that manner. However, the accessory equipment must be locked in place for transport to ensure that neither the accessories nor the equipment itself shifts during transport.

Question: A tractor loader-backhoe weighing over 10,000 pounds is being transported on a trailer. The loader and backhoe accessories are each equipped with locking devices or mechanisms that prevent them from moving up and down and from side-to-side while the construction equipment is being transported on the trailer. Must these accessories also be secured to the trailer with chains?

Guidance: No. However, if the construction equipment does not have a means of preventing the loader bucket, backhoe, or similar accessories from moving while it is being transported on the trailer, then a chain would be required to secure those accessories to the trailer.

3.8 Heavy Vehicles, Equipment, and Machinery

3.9 Flattened or Crushed Vehicles

Securement requirements 110
Transport vehicle options 110
Containing loose parts 112

The requirements in this chapter apply to the transportation of vehicles such as automobiles, light trucks, and vans that have been flattened or crushed.

3.9 Flattened or Crushed Vehicles

Securement requirements

- Transport flattened or crushed vehicles so that:
  - Cargo does not shift while in transit, AND
  - Loose parts from the flattened vehicles do not dislodge and fall from the transport vehicle.
- Do not use synthetic webbing to secure vehicles directly.
- Webbing may be used to connect wire rope or chain to anchor points on the vehicle, but the webbing (regardless of whether edge protection is used) must not contact the flattened or crushed vehicles.

 Canadian rules do not contain a provision allowing webbing to be used for connecting rope or chain to the vehicle.

Transport vehicle options

Secure flattened or crushed vehicles on a vehicle that meets one of the following four options.

Option #1

Has containment walls (or comparable) on four sides that:

- Extend to the full height of the load, AND
- Block against cargo movement in the forward, rearward, and sideways directions.

Option #2

Has containment walls (or comparable) on three sides that:

- Extend to the full height of the load, AND
- Block against cargo movement in the direction for which there is a wall or comparable means of containment.

Secure each stack of vehicles with a minimum of two tiedowns.

3.9 Flattened or Crushed Vehicles

Option #3

Has containment walls on two sides that:

- Extend to the full height of the load, AND
- Block against cargo movement in the forward and rearward directions.

Secure each stack of vehicles with a minimum of three tiedowns.

Option #4

Has a minimum of four tiedowns per vehicle stack.

 Each tiedown used for options 2, 3, and 4 must have a WLL of at least 2,268 kg (5,000 lb.).

 More tiedowns may be required to satisfy the general cargo securement requirement that the sum of the working load limits from all tiedowns must be at least 50% of the weight of the cargo.

Prohibited use of straps

3.9 Flattened or Crushed Vehicles

Containing loose parts

Use a containment system that:

- Prevents liquids from leaking from the bottom of the vehicle, AND
- Prevents loose parts from falling from the bottom and all four sides of the vehicle, extending to the full height of the cargo.

The containment system can consist of one or a combination of the following methods:

- Structural walls.
- Sides or sideboards.
- Suitable covering material.

The use of synthetic material for containment of loose parts is permitted.

3.10 Roll-On/Roll-Off and Hook-Lift Containers

Container securement requirements 114

The requirements in this chapter apply to the transportation of roll-on/roll-off and hook-lift containers.

Generally, roll-on/roll-off and hook-lift containers are carried on specially designed vehicles that are equipped with securing devices on the vehicle. When the container is secured, it combines the container and the vehicle into one unit.

3.10 Roll-On/Roll-Off and Hook-Lift Containers

This chapter deals with how to transport a container on a vehicle that is **not** equipped with a compatible and functioning "Integral Securement System."

 An integral securement system is a system on certain roll-on/roll-off containers and hook-lift containers and their related transport vehicles in which compatible front and rear hold-down devices are mated to provide securement of the complete vehicle and its articles of cargo.

Container securement requirements

- Block against forward movement by the lifting device, stops, a combination of both, or another suitable restraint mechanism.

- Secure to the front of the vehicle by the lifting device or another suitable restraint to prevent side-to-side and vertical movement.

- Secure to the rear of the vehicle with at least ONE of the following three mechanisms:

    - <u>Mechanism #1</u>: One tiedown attached to both the vehicle chassis and the container chassis.

3.10 Roll-On/Roll-Off and Hook-Lift Containers

- **Mechanism #2**: Two tiedowns installed lengthwise, each securing one side of the container to one of the vehicle's side rails.
- **Mechanism #3**: Two hooks, or an equivalent mechanism, securing both sides of the container to the vehicle chassis at least as effectively as the tiedowns in the two previous items.

• Attach mechanisms used to secure the rear end of a roll-on/roll-off or hook-lift container no more than 6 feet 7 inches (2 m) from the rear of the container.

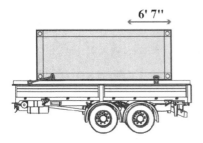

 Each mechanism must have a WLL of at least 2,268 kg (5,000 lb.).

• Manually install additional tiedowns if one or more of the front stops or lifting devices is missing, damaged, or not compatible.

 Manually installed tiedowns must provide the same level of securement as the missing, damaged, or incompatible components.

3.10 Roll-On/Roll-Off and Hook-Lift Containers

3.11 Boulders

Positioning boulders	119
Tiedown requirements	121
Securing a cubic-shaped boulder	122
Securing a non-cubic shaped boulder with a stable base	122
Securing a non-cubic shaped boulder with an unstable base	123

The requirements in this chapter apply to any piece of natural, irregularly shaped rock that:

- Weighs more than 11,000 pounds (5,000 kg) or has a volume greater than two cubic meters.
- Is transported on an open vehicle or in a vehicle whose sides are not designed and rated for the transportation of boulders.

117

3.11 Boulders

Two cubic meters is about the size of a box with dimensions of 4 feet (1.25 m) on every side.

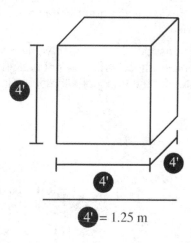

Boulders weighing less than 11,000 pounds (5,000 kg) may be secured in one of two ways:

1. Using the requirements for large boulders (this chapter).

2. In some situations, using the general cargo securement requirements if:

    - Transported in a vehicle designed to carry boulders.

    - Boulders are stabilized and adequately secured by tiedowns (each piece must be stabilized and secured).

Rock that is formed or cut to shape and has a stable base can be secured either by:

- The requirements for large boulders, OR
- The requirements for general cargo.

3.11 Boulders

Positioning boulders

- Place each boulder on the vehicle with its flattest and/or largest side down.

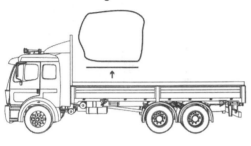

- Support each boulder on at least two pieces of 4 x 4 inch (8.9 cm) hardwood blocking that extends the full width of the boulder.
- Place hardwood blocking pieces as symmetrically as possible under the boulder so they support at least 3/4 of the length of the boulder.

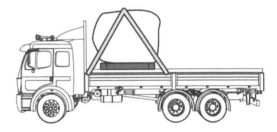

3.11 Boulders

- If the flattest side of the boulder is rounded or partially rounded, place the boulder in a crib made of hardwood and fixed to the deck of the vehicle.

    - The boulder should rest on both the deck and the timber, with at least 3 well-separated points of contact that prevent rolling in any direction.

- If a boulder is tapered, point the narrowest end towards the front of the vehicle.

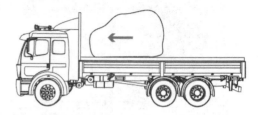

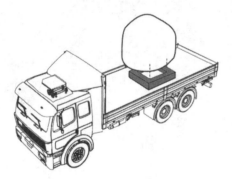

3.11 Boulders

Tiedown requirements

- Use only <u>chain</u> to secure large boulders.

- Tiedowns in direct contact with the boulder:
  - Should be located in valleys or notches across the top of the boulder, when possible.
  - Must be arranged to prevent sliding across the rock surface.

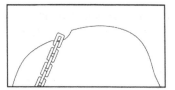

3.11 Boulders

Securing a cubic-shaped boulder

The securement of a cubic-shaped boulder must meet these requirements in addition to the other large boulder requirements in this chapter.

- Secure each boulder individually with at least two chain tiedowns placed side-to-side across the vehicle.
- Place tiedowns as closely as possible to the hardwood blocking used to support the boulder.

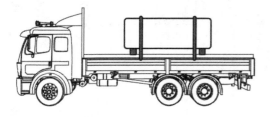

> The aggregate WLL of the tiedowns must be at least 50% of the weight of the boulder.

Securing a non-cubic shaped boulder with a stable base

The securement of a non-cubic shaped boulder with a stable base must meet these requirements in addition to the other large boulder requirements in this chapter.

- Secure each boulder individually with at least two chain tiedowns forming an "X" pattern over the boulder.
- Pass the tiedowns over the center of the boulder and attach them to each other at the intersection by a shackle or other connecting device.

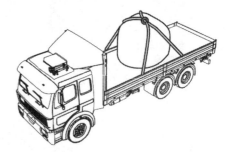

3.11 Boulders

Securing a non-cubic shaped boulder with an unstable base

The securement of a non-cubic shaped boulder with an unstable base must meet these requirements in addition to the other large boulder requirements in this chapter.

- Surround the top of each boulder at a point between 1/2 and 2/3 of its height with one chain.

The WLL of the chain must be at least 50% of the weight of the boulder.

- Attach four chains to the surrounding chain and the vehicle to form a blocking mechanism that prevents any horizontal movement.

The WLL of these chains must be at least 25% of the weight of the boulder, and the angle must be less than 45° from the horizontal.

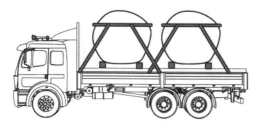

3.11 Boulders

3.12 Square Bales of Hay and Straw

Background 126
Loading pattern 127
Securement 127

The requirements in this chapter apply to the transportation of square bales of hay and straw.

 This chapter is based on a U.S. policy that has not yet been adopted into the Canadian National Safety Code. Unless and until that happens, drivers transporting hay in Canada must continue to follow the general cargo securement rules. Provincial requirements may vary.

3.12 Square Bales of Hay and Straw

Background

The securement standards in this chapter are not based on the regulations themselves, but rather a September 28, 2007, memorandum from the U.S. Federal Motor Carrier Safety Administration to enforcement personnel. The memo states that, after reviewing a series of tests, the agency concluded that the cargo securement requirements for square bales can be met by using longstanding industry practices involving the use of fewer tiedowns than the regulations would otherwise require. Those longstanding practices — which in some cases have been adopted into state law — employ a combination of longitudinal tiedowns and a loading pattern that interlocks adjacent bales together.

> Though the FMCSA has asked the states to avoid penalizing carriers that use the newly-approved securement method, not all states may follow that recommendation. Motor carriers should check with their states for current enforcement practices.

According to the memo, the test results "demonstrate conclusively that the combination of longitudinal tiedown assemblies and a loading pattern that effectively unitizes the bales of hay and straw, along with the addition of one or two lateral cargo securement devices depending on vehicle length, provides a securement system that meets or exceeds the performance criteria established by the [federal regulations] and does not result in any degradation in the level of safety during transport."

The memo does not specify a size for the individual bales.

3.12 Square Bales of Hay and Straw

Loading pattern

The square bales should be loaded in a pattern which interlocks adjacent bales together, thereby helping to "unitize" the load so that the bales effectively act as a single unit.

Securement

Loads of square bales of hay and straw will satisfy the "equivalent means of securement" standard (49 CFR §393.102(c)) and will be considered to be adequately secured if:

1. The load is unitized using longitudinal (front to back) ropes or tiedown assemblies;

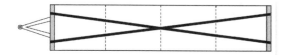

If the load is not unitized and secured according to these standards, then the "general" cargo securement rules (section 2 of this handbook) would apply.

2. The sum of the working load limits of all tiedowns is at least 50% of the weight of the cargo;

3. At least one lateral (side to side) tiedown is placed in the approximate center of the length of the any truck or trailer 32 feet or less in length; and

4. At least two lateral tiedowns are placed at approximately one-third and two-thirds of the length of any truck or trailer greater than 32 feet long.

3.12 Square Bales of Hay and Straw

4. REFERENCE
4.1 Frequently Asked Questions (FAQs)

Are tarps required?

They are not specifically required under the federal rules, but they may be necessary to contain certain types of loads, and some states, provinces, and/or your company may require their use.

Can cargo straps go around the outside of the rub rails?

Yes, in the U.S., but not in Canada. At least as a best practice, all straps should be routed inboard of the rub rails whenever possible.

Do I have to secure cargo in my dry van?

Yes, all cargo and equipment must be secured against movement, regardless of vehicle type.

We haul heavy equipment. Do accessories like hydraulic buckets, shovels, and blades have to be secured?

Yes, you must completely lower and secure all accessory equipment to the vehicle. Refer to chapter 3.8.

4.1 Frequently Asked Questions (FAQs)

Does coiled wire have to be secured according to the rules for metal coils?

In the U.S., yes, all coiled, rolled, or wrapped metal objects must be secured according to the rules for metal coils. In Canada, the rules for metal coils apply only to coils of rolled sheet metal.

Do I have to secure my spare tire, spare chains, landing gear crank, and other vehicle equipment?

Yes. The tailgate, tailboard, dunnage, doors, tarps, spare tire, straps, chains, binders, wood blocks, and other equipment used in the vehicle's operation must be secured.

Does my vehicle have to have a headerboard/bull board/headache rack?

No. But if your cargo is in contact with a front end structure, then that structure must comply with certain specifications. In the U.S. regulations, refer to 49 CFR 393.114.

4.2 CVSA North American Standard Vehicle Out-of-Service Criteria: Cargo Securement

The following is a portion of the Commercial Vehicle Safety Alliance's *North American Standard Vehicle Out-of-Service Criteria*. It identifies critical vehicle inspection items related to cargo securement and provides criteria for placing vehicles out of service due to loading conditions that are likely to cause an accident or breakdown. To order the official *CVSA North American Standard Out-of-Service Criteria*, visit www.cvsa.org.

SAFE LOADING/TIE-DOWNS

a. Part(s) of a vehicle or condition of loading such that the spare tire or any part of the load, cargo or dunnage can fall onto the roadway. (392.9)

b. When the aggregate working load limit of the securement devices being used is less than $1/2$ the weight of the cargo being secured. (393.106(d))

   NOTE: Equivalent means of securement (e.g., vehicle structures, dunnage, dunnage bags, shoring bars, etc.) may be used to comply; not all cargo must be "tied down" with chains, webbing, wire rope, cordage, etc. (393.106(b))

c. No edge protection. (393.104(f)(5))

   NOTE: Out-of-Service <u>only</u> when the required tie-down has evidence of damage resulting from unprotected contact with an article of cargo.

   NOTE: See items 7.h.(1) through 7.h.(5) for tie-down defect classification.

d. Articles of cargo that are likely to roll are not restrained by chocks, wedges, a cradle or other equivalent means to prevent rolling. (393.106(c)(1)) for all types of cargo including light-weight vehicles, 393.130(a) for heavy vehicles, equipment and machinery.)

e. Articles or cargo placed beside each other and secured by transverse tie-downs are not in direct contact with each other and are not prevented from shifting towards each other while in transit. (393.106(c)(2))

f. Articles or cargo not blocked or positioned to prevent movement in the forward direction by a headerboard, bulkhead, other cargo that is positioned to prevent movement, or other appropriate blocking devices, is not secured by at least:

   (1) One tie-down for articles 5 feet (1.52m) or less in length, and 1,100 pounds (500kg) or less in weight. (393.110(b)(1));

   (2) Two tie-downs if the article is:

   (a) 5 feet (1.52m) or less in length and more than 1,100 pounds (500kg) in weight (393.110(b)(2)(i)); or

   (b) Longer than 5 feet (1.52m) but less than or equal to 10 feet (3.04m) in length, irrespective of the weight. (393.110(b)(2)(ii))

4.2 CVSA North American Standard Vehicle Out-of-Service Criteria: Cargo Securement

    (3) Two tie-downs if the article is longer than 10 feet (3.04m) and one additional tie-down for every 10 feet (3.04m) of article length, or fraction thereof, beyond the first 10 feet (3.04m) of length. (393.110(b)(3))

g. Article(s) or cargo that is blocked, braced or immobilized to prevent movement in the forward direction by a headerboard, bulkhead, other articles which are adequately secured or by an appropriate blocking or immobilization method, is not secured by at least one tie-down for every 10 feet (3.04m) of article length, or fraction thereof. (393.110(c))

h. When any of the required type and number of tie-downs are defective or loose. (393.104(b) — Defective, 393.104(f) — Loose)

    (1) Chain Defects

        (a) Broken, cracked, twisted, bent, or stretched links. (393.104(b))

        (b) Containing nicks, gouges, abrasions, excessive wear, or knots. (393.104(b))

        (c) Any weld(s) on chain, except the original chain weld in each link. (393.104(f)(2))

NOTE: Repairs. Links of the clevis variety, having a strength equal to or greater than the nominal chain are acceptable. (See also Tie-Down Guidelines.)

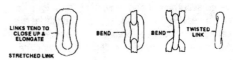

    (2) Wire Rope Defects

        (a) Kinks, bird caging, popped core, or knots in the working section of the wire rope. (393.104(b), 393.104(f)(1))

        (b) Discoloration from excessive heat or electric arc in the eye or main body of the wire rope. (393.104(b))

        (c) Corrosion with pitting of the external or internal wires. (393.104(b))

        (d) More than 11 broken wires in 6 diameters of length. For example: with $1/2$ inch (13mm) wire rope, over 11 broken wires in (6 x $1/2$) or 3 inches in length. (6 x 13 = 78mm). (393.104(b))

        (e) More than three broken wires in any one strand. (393.104(b))

        (f) More than two broken wires at the end connection or fitting. (393.104(b))

4.2 CVSA North American Standard Vehicle Out-of-Service Criteria: Cargo Securement

NOTE: Repairs. Wire rope used in tie-down assemblies shall not be repaired or spliced. (Back splices and eye splices are acceptable.)

Examples of Bird Cages

Rope Kink

Examples of Core Protrusion

(3) Cordage (fiber rope) Defects

  (a) Burned or melted fibers except on heat-sealed ends. (393.104(b))

  (b) *Evidence of excessive wear in exterior or interior fibers. (393.104(b))

  (c) *Any evidence of loss of strength, such as a marked reduction in diameter. (393.104(b))

  (d) Ineffective knots formed for the purpose of connecting or repairing binders. (393.104(f)(1))

*NOTE: Effective diameter of cordage reduced by 20 percent is excessive. Repairs: Cordage used in tie-down assemblies shall not be repaired. (Separate lengths of cordage properly spliced together are not considered repairs.)

(4) Synthetic Webbing

  (a) The tie-down contains cut(s), burn(s), and/or hole(s) through the webbing which total more than that shown in the Defect Classification Table. (393.104(b))

  (b) The tie-down contains separation of its load carrying stitch pattern(s) in excess of $1/4$ of the total stitch area. (393.104(b))

  (c) The tie-down contains any fitting, tensioning device, or hardware which is broken, obviously sprung, bent, twisted, or contains visible cracks or significant nicks or gouges. (393.104(b))

  (d) The tie-down contains knotted webbing splices, repairs, or any other apparent defects (i.e., crushed areas, damaged loop ends, severe abrasions, etc.). (393.104(b), 393.104(f)(2))

4.2 CVSA North American Standard Vehicle Out-of-Service Criteria: Cargo Securement

DEFECT CLASSIFICATION TABLE
Total Defect Size

Web Size Inches (mm)	Out-of-Service Range Inches (mm)
4 (100)	Larger than $3/4$ (19)
3 (75)	Larger than $5/8$ (16)
2 (50)	Larger than $3/8$ (10)
1.75 (45)	Larger than $3/8$ (10)

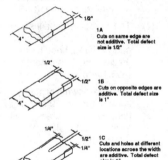

1A Cuts on same edge are not additive. Total defect size is 1/2"

1B Cuts on opposite edges are additive. Total defect size is 1"

1C Cuts and holes at different locations across the width are additive. Total defect size is 1"

All cut(s), burn(s), and/or hole(s) through the webbing are additive across the width of the strap face for its entire effective length. But only one defect is additive for any specific width.

NOTE: Repairs. Webbing used in tie-down assemblies shall not be repaired or spliced.

(5) Steel Strapping

(a) Steel strappings over one inch (25mm) in width not having at least two pair of crimps in each seal. (393.104(e))

(b) Steel strappings arranged in an end-over-end lap joint not sealed with at least two seals. (393.104(e))

(c) Obviously damaged or distorted steel strappings. (393.104(b))

(6) Fitting or Attachment Defects

(a) Obvious reduction of section through wear or corrosion. (393.104(b))

(b) Obviously distorted or stretched load binders and fittings. (393.104(b))

(c) Hooks opened in the throat beyond the original parallel throat opening. (393.104(b))

(d) Obvious twisting out of the plane of the fitting. (393.104(b))

4.2 CVSA North American Standard Vehicle Out-of-Service Criteria: Cargo Securement

      (e) Welding or discoloration from excessive heat. (393.104(b))

      NOTE: Some winches are designed to be welded to the truck bed.

      (f) Any visible cracks. (393.104(b))

      (g) Any slippage detectable at a wire rope "cable clamp". (393.104(f)(2))

      NOTE: End fittings may be replaced with clevis type.

  (7) Anchor Point Defects

      (a) Broken or cracked side or pocket rails, supports, or welds. (393.104(c))

      (b) Rails bent or distorted where hooks or fittings attach. (393.104(c))

      (c) Floor rings nicked, gouged, worn, twisted, bent, stretched, or with broken welds. (393.104(c))

i. Logs not secured per the specific securement requirements for this commodity type. (393.116)

j. Dressed lumber or similar building products not secured per the specific securement requirements for this commodity type. (393.118)

k. Metal coils not secured per the specific securement requirements for this commodity type. (393.120)

l. Paper rolls not secured per the specific securement requirements for this commodity type. (393.122)

m. Concrete pipe not secured per the specific securement requirements for this commodity type. (393.124)

n. Intermodal containers not secured per the specific securement requirements for this commodity type. (393.126)

o. Automobiles, light trucks and vans not secured per the specific securement requirements for this commodity type. (393.128)

p. Heavy vehicles, equipment and machinery not secured per the specific securement requirements for this commodity type. (393.130)

q. Flattened or crushed vehicles not secured per the specific securement requirements for this commodity type. (393.132)

r. Roll-On/Roll-Off or Hook Lift Containers not secured per the specific securement requirements for this commodity type. (393.134)

s. Large boulders not secured per the specific securement requirements for this commodity type. (393.136)

4.2 CVSA North American Standard Vehicle Out-of-Service Criteria: Cargo Securement

4.3 Cargo Securement Regulations

Canadian Rules: The Canadian cargo securement standard is known as *National Safety Code Standard 10, Cargo Securement*. The Standard is only available from the Canadian Council of Motor Transport Administrators (CCMTA).

CCMTA
2323 St. Laurent Blvd.
Ottawa, Ontario K1G 4J8
Canada
Telephone: (613) 736-1003
Fax: (613) 736-1395
E-mail: ccmta-secretariat@ccmta.ca
Web site: www.ccmta.ca

U.S. Rules: The U.S. cargo securement rules from 49 CFR §392.9 and Part 393, Subpart I, are as follows:

§392.9 Inspection of cargo, cargo securement devices and systems.

(a) **General.** A driver may not operate a commercial motor vehicle and a motor carrier may not require or permit a driver to operate a commercial motor vehicle unless—

(1) The commercial motor vehicle's cargo is properly distributed and adequately secured as specified in §§393.100 through 393.142 of this subchapter;

(2) The commercial motor vehicle's tailgate, tailboard, doors, tarpaulins, spare tire and other equipment used in its operation, and the means of fastening the commercial motor vehicle's cargo, are secured; and

(3) The commercial motor vehicle's cargo or any other object does not obscure the driver's view ahead or to the right or left sides (except for drivers of self-steer dollies), interfere with the free movement of his/her arms or legs, prevent his/her free and ready access to accessories required for emergencies, or prevent the free and ready exit of any person from the commercial motor vehicle's cab or driver's compartment.

(b) **Drivers of trucks and truck tractors.** Except as provided in paragraph (b)(4) of this section, the driver of a truck or truck tractor must—

4.3 Cargo Securement Regulations

(1) Assure himself/herself that the provisions of paragraph (a) of this section have been complied with before he/she drives that commercial motor vehicle;

(2) Inspect the cargo and the devices used to secure the cargo within the first 50 miles after beginning a trip and cause any adjustments to be made to the cargo or load securement devices as necessary, including adding more securement devices, to ensure that cargo cannot shift on or within, or fall from the commercial motor vehicle; and

(3) Reexamine the commercial motor vehicle's cargo and its load securement devices during the course of transportation and make any necessary adjustment to the cargo or load securement devices, including adding more securement devices, to ensure that cargo cannot shift on or within, or fall from, the commercial motor vehicle. Reexamination and any necessary adjustments must be made whenever—

(i) The driver makes a change of his/her duty status; or

(ii) The commercial motor vehicle has been driven for 3 hours; or

(iii) The commercial motor vehicle has been driven for 150 miles, whichever occurs first.

(4) The rules in this paragraph (b) do not apply to the driver of a sealed commercial motor vehicle who has been ordered not to open it to inspect its cargo or to the driver of a commercial motor vehicle that has been loaded in a manner that makes inspection of its cargo impracticable.

Subpart I – Protection Against Shifting or Falling Cargo

393.100   Which types of commercial motor vehicles are subject to the cargo securement standards of this subpart, and what general requirements apply?

393.102   What are the minimum performance criteria for cargo securement devices and systems?

393.104   What standards must cargo securement devices and systems meet in order to satisfy the requirements of this subpart?

393.106   What are the general requirements for securing articles of cargo?

393.108   How is the working load limit of a tiedown, or the load restraining value of a friction mat, determined?

393.110   What else do I have do to determine the minimum number of tiedowns?

393.112   Must a tiedown be adjustable?

393.114   What are the requirements for front end structures used as part of a cargo securement system?

Specific Securement Requirements by Commodity Type

393.116   What are the rules for securing logs?

393.118   What are the rules for securing dressed lumber or similar building products?

393.120   What are the rules for securing metal coils?

4.3 Cargo Securement Regulations

393.122 What are the rules for securing paper rolls?

393.124 What are the rules for securing concrete pipe?

393.126 What are the rules for securing intermodal containers?

393.128 What are the rules for securing automobiles, light trucks and vans?

393.130 What are the rules for securing heavy vehicles, equipment and machinery?

393.132 What are the rules for securing flattened or crushed vehicles?

393.134 What are the rules for securing roll-on/roll-off or hook lift containers?

393.136 What are the rules for securing large boulders?

§393.100 Which types of commercial motor vehicles are subject to the cargo securement standards of this subpart, and what general requirements apply?

(a) **Applicability.** The rules in this subpart are applicable to trucks, truck tractors, semitrailers, full trailers, and pole trailers.

(b) **Prevention against loss of load.** Each commercial motor vehicle must, when transporting cargo on public roads, be loaded and equipped, and the cargo secured, in accordance with this subpart to prevent the cargo from leaking, spilling, blowing or falling from the motor vehicle.

(c) **Prevention against shifting of load.** Cargo must be contained, immobilized or secured in accordance with this subpart to prevent shifting upon or within the vehicle to such an extent that the vehicle's stability or maneuverability is adversely affected.

§393.102 What are the minimum performance criteria for cargo securement devices and systems?

(a) **Performance criteria**–(1) Breaking Strength. Tiedown assemblies (including chains, wire rope, steel strapping, synthetic webbing, and cordage) and other attachment or fastening devices used to secure articles of cargo to, or in, commercial motor vehicles must be designed, installed, and maintained to ensure that the maximum forces acting on the devices or systems do not exceed the manufacturer's breaking strength rating under the following conditions, applied separately:

(i) 0.8 g deceleration in the forward direction;

(ii) 0.5 g acceleration in the rearward direction; and

(iii) 0.5 g acceleration in a lateral direction.

(2) **Working Load Limit.** Tiedown assemblies (including chains, wire rope, steel strapping, synthetic webbing, and cordage) and other attachment or fastening devices used to secure articles of cargo to, or in, commercial motor vehicles must be designed, installed, and maintained to ensure that the forces acting on the devices or systems do not exceed the

4.3 Cargo Securement Regulations

working load limit for the devices under the following conditions, applied separately:

(i) 0.435 g deceleration in the forward direction;

(ii) 0.5 g acceleration in the rearward direction; and

(iii) 0.25 g acceleration in a lateral direction.

(b) **Performance criteria for devices to prevent vertical movement of loads that are not contained within the structure of the vehicle.** Securement systems must provide a downward force equivalent to at least 20 percent of the weight of the article of cargo if the article is not fully contained within the structure of the vehicle. If the article is fully contained within the structure of the vehicle, it may be secured in accordance with §393.106(b).

(c) **Equivalent means of securement.** The means of securing articles of cargo are considered to meet the performance requirements of this section if the cargo is:

(1) Immobilized, such so that it cannot shift or tip to the extent that the vehicle's stability or maneuverability is adversely affected; or

(2) Transported in a sided vehicle that has walls of adequate strength, such that each article of cargo within the vehicle is in contact with, or sufficiently close to a wall or other articles, so that it cannot shift or tip to the extent that the vehicle's stability or maneuverability is adversely affected; or

(3) Secured in accordance with the applicable requirements of §§393.104 through 393.136.

§393.104 What standards must cargo securement devices and systems meet in order to satisfy the requirements of this subpart?

(a) **General.** All devices and systems used to secure cargo to or within a vehicle must be capable of meeting the requirements of §393.102.

(b) **Prohibition on the use of damaged securement devices.** All tiedowns, cargo securement systems, parts and components used to secure cargo must be in proper working order when used to perform that function with no damaged or weakened components, such as, but not limited to, cracks or cuts that will adversely affect their performance for cargo securement purposes, including reducing the working load limit.

(c) **Vehicle structures and anchor points.** Vehicle structures, floors, walls, decks, tiedown anchor points, headerboards, bulkheads, stakes, posts, and associated mounting pockets used to contain or secure articles of cargo must be strong enough to meet the performance criteria of §393.102, with no damaged or weakened components, such as, but not limited to, cracks or cuts that will adversely affect their performance for cargo securement purposes, including reducing the working load limit.

(d) **Material for dunnage, chocks, cradles, shoring bars, blocking and bracing.** Material used as dunnage or dunnage bags, chocks, cradles, shoring bars, or used for blocking and bracing, must not have damage or defects which

4.3 Cargo Securement Regulations

would compromise the effectiveness of the securement system.

(e) **Manufacturing standards for tiedown assemblies.** Tiedown assemblies (including chains, wire rope, steel strapping, synthetic webbing, and cordage) and other attachment or fastening devices used to secure articles of cargo to, or in, commercial motor vehicles must conform to the following applicable standards:

An assembly component of . . .	Must conform to . . .
(1) Steel strapping[1,2]	Standard Specification for Strapping, Flat Steel and Seals, American Society for Testing and Materials (ASTM) D3953-97, February 1998.[4]
(2) Chain	National Association of Chain Manufacturers' Welded Steel Chain Specifications, dated September 28, 2005.[4]
(3) Webbing	Web Sling and Tiedown Association's Recommended Standard Specification for Synthetic Web Tiedowns, WSTDA-T1, 1998.[4]
(4) Wire rope[3]	Wire Rope Technical Board's Wire Rope Users Manual, 2nd Edition, November 1985.[4]

An assembly component of . . .	Must conform to . . .
(5) Cordage	Cordage Institute rope standard: (i) PETRS-2, Polyester Fiber Rope, three-Strand and eight-Strand Constructions, January 1993;[4] (ii) PPRS-2, Polypropylene Fiber Rope, three-Strand and eight-Strand Constructions, August 1992;[4] (iii) CRS-1, Polyester/Polypropylene Composite Rope Specifications, three-Strand and eight-Strand Standard Construction, May 1979;[4] (iv) NRS-1, Nylon Rope Specifications, three-Strand and eight-Strand Standard Construction, May 1979;[4] and (v) C-1, Double Braided Nylon Rope Specifications DBN, January 1984.[4]

[1] Steel strapping not marked by the manufacturer with a working load limit will be considered to have a working load limit equal to one-fourth of the breaking strength listed in ASTM D3953-97.

[2] Steel strapping 25.4 mm (1 inch) or wider must have at least two pairs of crimps in each seal and, when an end-over-end lap joint is formed, must be sealed with at least two seals.

[3] Wire rope which is not marked by the manufacturer with a working load limit shall be considered to have a working load limit equal to one-fourth of the nominal strength listed in the manual.

[4] See §393.7 for information on the incorporation by reference and availability of this document.

(f) **Use of tiedowns.** (1) Tiedowns and securing devices must not contain knots.

4.3 Cargo Securement Regulations

(2) If a tiedown is repaired, it must be repaired in accordance with the applicable standards in paragraph (e) of this section, or the manufacturer's instructions.

(3) Each tiedown must be attached and secured in a manner that prevents it from becoming loose, unfastening, opening or releasing while the vehicle is in transit.

(4) Edge protection must be used whenever a tiedown would be subject to abrasion or cutting at the point where it touches an article of cargo. The edge protection must resist abrasion, cutting and crushing.

§393.106 What are the general requirements for securing articles of cargo?

(a) **Applicability.** The rules in this section are applicable to the transportation of all types of articles of cargo, except commodities in bulk that lack structure or fixed shape (*e.g.*, liquids, gases, grain, liquid concrete, sand, gravel, aggregates) and are transported in a tank, hopper, box, or similar device that forms part of the structure of a commercial motor vehicle. The rules in this section apply to the cargo types covered by the commodity-specific rules of §393.116 through §393.136. The commodity-specific rules take precedence over the general requirements of this section when additional requirements are given for a commodity listed in those sections.

(b) **General.** Cargo must be firmly immobilized or secured on or within a vehicle by structures of adequate strength, dunnage or dunnage bags, shoring bars, tiedowns or a combination of these.

(c) **Cargo placement and restraint.** (1) Articles of cargo that are likely to roll must be restrained by chocks, wedges, a cradle or other equivalent means to prevent rolling. The means of preventing rolling must not be capable of becoming unintentionally unfastened or loose while the vehicle is in transit.

(2) Articles or cargo placed beside each other and secured by transverse tiedowns must either:

(i) Be placed in direct contact with each other, or

(ii) Be prevented from shifting towards each other while in transit.

(d) **Aggregate working load limit for tiedowns.** The aggregate working load limit of tiedowns used to secure an article or group of articles against movement must be at least one-half times the weight of the article or group of articles. The aggregate working load limit is the sum of:

(1) One-half the working load limit of each tiedown that goes from an anchor point on the vehicle to an anchor point on an article of cargo;

(2) One-half the working load limit of each tiedown that is attached to an anchor point on the vehicle, passes through, over, or around the article of cargo, and is then attached to an anchor point on the same side of the vehicle.

(3) The working load limit for each tiedown that goes from an anchor point on the vehicle, through, over, or around the article of cargo, and then attaches to another anchor point on the other side of the vehicle.

4.3 Cargo Securement Regulations

§393.108 How is the working load limit of a tiedown, or the load restraining value of a friction mat, determined?

(a) The working load limit (WLL) of a tiedown, associated connector or attachment mechanism is the lowest working load limit of any of its components (including tensioner), or the working load limit of the anchor points to which it is attached, whichever is less.

(b) The working load limits of tiedowns may be determined by using either the tiedown manufacturer's markings or by using the tables in this section. The working load limits listed in the tables are to be used when the tiedown material is not marked by the manufacturer with the working load limit. Tiedown materials which are marked by the manufacturer with working load limits that differ from the tables, shall be considered to have a working load limit equal to the value for which they are marked.

(c) Synthetic cordage (*e.g.*, nylon, polypropylene, polyester) which is not marked or labeled to enable identification of its composition or working load limit shall be considered to have a working load limit equal to that for polypropylene fiber rope.

(d) Welded steel chain which is not marked or labeled to enable identification of its grade or working load limit shall be considered to have a working load limit equal to that for grade 30 proof coil chain.

(e)(1) Wire rope which is not marked by the manufacturer with a working load limit shall be considered to have a working load limit equal to one-fourth of the nominal strength listed in the Wire Rope Users Manual.

(2) Wire which is not marked or labeled to enable identification of its construction type shall be considered to have a working load limit equal to that for 6 x 37, fiber core wire rope.

(f) Manila rope which is not marked by the manufacturer with a working load limit shall be considered to have a working load limit based on its diameter as provided in the tables of working load limits.

(g) Friction mats which are not marked or rated by the manufacturer shall be considered to provide resistance to horizontal movement equal to 50 percent of the weight placed on the mat.

4.3 Cargo Securement Regulations

Tables to §393.108
[Working Load Limits (WLL), Chain]

Size mm (inches)	WLL in kg (pounds)				
	Grade 30 proof coil	Grade 43 high test	Grade 70 transport	Grade 80 alloy	Grade 100 alloy
1. 7 ($^1/_4$)	580 (1,300)	1,180 (2,600)	1,430 (3,150)	1,570 (3,500)	1,950 (4,300)
2. 8 ($^5/_{16}$)	860 (1,900)	1,770 (3,900)	2,130 (4,700)	2,000 (4,500)	2,600 (5,700)
3. 10 ($^3/_8$)	1,200 (2,650)	2,450 (5,400)	2,990 (6,600)	3,200 (7,100)	4,000 (8,800)
4. 11 ($^7/_{16}$)	1,680 (3,700)	3,270 (7,200)	3,970 (8,750)		
5. 13 ($^1/_2$)	2,030 (4,500)	4,170 (9,200)	5,130 (11,300)	5,400 (12,000)	6,800 (15,000)
6. 16 ($^5/_8$)	3,130 (6,900)	5,910 (13,000)	7,170 (15,800)	8,200 (18,100)	10,300 (22,600)
Chain Mark Examples:					
Example 1	3	4	7	8	10
Example 2	30	43	70	80	100
Example 3	300	430	700	800	1000

Editor's Note: The working load limits for 5/16" grade 70 and grade 80 chain are correct as shown. Due to differences in nominal and actual chain sizes, 5/16" grade 70 chain has a slightly higher WLL than 5/16" grade 80 chain.

Synthetic Webbing

Width mm (inches)	WLL kg (pounds)
45 (1 ¾)	790 (1,750)
50 (2)	910 (2,000)
75 (3)	1,360 (3,000)
100 (4)	1,810 (4,000)

Wire Rope (6 x 37, Fiber Core)

Diameter mm (inches)	WLL kg (pounds)
7 ($^1/_4$)	640 (1,400)
8 ($^5/_{16}$)	950 (2,100)
10 ($^3/_8$)	1,360 (3,000)
11 ($^7/_{16}$)	1,860 (4,100)
13 ($^1/_2$)	2,400 (5,300)
16 ($^5/_8$)	3,770 (8,300)
20 ($^3/_4$)	4,940 (10,900)
22 ($^7/_8$)	7,300 (16,100)
25 (1)	9,480 (20,900)

4.3 Cargo Securement Regulations

Manila Rope

Diameter mm (inches)	WLL kg (pounds)
10 ($^3/_8$)	90 (205)
11 ($^7/_{16}$)	120 (265)
13 ($^1/_2$)	150 (315)
16 ($^5/_8$)	210 (465)
20 ($^3/_4$)	290 (640)
25 (1)	480 (1,050)

Polypropylene Fiber Rope WLL
(3-Strand and 8-Strand Constructions)

Diameter mm (inches)	WLL kg (pounds)
10 ($^3/_8$)	180 (400)
11 ($^7/_{16}$)	240 (525)
13 ($^1/_2$)	280 (625)
16 ($^5/_8$)	420 (925)
20 ($^3/_4$)	580 (1,275)
25 (1)	950 (2,100)

Polyester Fiber Rope WLL
(3-Strand and 8-Strand Constructions)

Diameter mm (inches)	WLL kg (pounds)
10 ($^3/_8$)	250 (555)
11 ($^7/_{16}$)	340 (750)
13 ($^1/_2$)	440 (960)
16 ($^5/_8$)	680 (1,500)
20 ($^3/_4$)	850 (1,880)
25 (1)	1,500 (3,300)

Nylon Rope

Diameter mm (inches)	WLL kg (pounds)
10 ($^3/_8$)	130 (278)
11 ($^7/_{16}$)	190 (410)
13 ($^1/_2$)	240 (525)
16 ($^5/_8$)	420 (935)
20 ($^3/_4$)	640 (1,420)
25 (1)	1,140 (2,520)

4.3 Cargo Securement Regulations

Double Braided Nylon Rope

Diameter mm (inches)	WLL kg (pounds)
10 (3/8)	150 (336)
11 (7/16)	230 (502)
13 (1/2)	300 (655)
16 (5/8)	510 (1,130)
20 (3/4)	830 (1,840)
25 (1)	1,470 (3,250)

Steel Strapping

Width x thickness mm (inches)	WLL kg (pounds)
31.7 x .74 (1 ¼ x 0.029)	540 (1,190)
31.7 x .79 (1 ¼ x 0.031)	540 (1,190)
31.7 x .89 (1 ¼ x 0.035)	540 (1,190)
31.7 x 1.12 (1 ¼ x 0.044)	770 (1,690)
31.7 x 1.27 (1 ¼ x 0.05)	770 (1,690)
31.7 x 1.5 (1 ¼ x 0.057)	870 (1,925)
50.8 x 1.12 (2 x 0.044)	1,200 (2,650)
50.8 x 1.27 (2 x 0.05)	1,200 (2,650)

§393.110 What else do I have to do to determine the minimum number of tiedowns?

(a) When tiedowns are used as part of a cargo securement system, the minimum number of tiedowns required to secure an article or group of articles against movement depends on the length of the article(s) being secured, and the requirements of paragraphs (b) and (c) of this section. These requirements are in addition to the rules under §393.106.

(b) When an article is not blocked or positioned to prevent movement in the forward direction by a headerboard, bulkhead, other cargo that is positioned to prevent movement, or other appropriate blocking devices, it must be secured by at least:

(1) One tiedown for articles 5 feet (1.52 meters) or less in length, and 1,100 pounds (500 kg) or less in weight;

(2) Two tiedowns if the article is:

(i) 5 feet (1.52 meters) or less in length and more than 1,100 pounds (500 kg) in weight; or

(ii) Longer than 5 feet (1.52 meters) but less than or equal to 10 feet (3.04 meters) in length, irrespective of the weight.

(3) Two tiedowns if the article is longer than 10 feet (3.04 meters), and one additional tiedown for every 10 feet (3.04 meters) of article length, or fraction thereof, beyond the first 10 feet (3.04 meters) of length.

(c) If an individual article is blocked, braced, or immobilized to prevent movement in the forward direction by a headerboard,

4.3 Cargo Securement Regulations

bulkhead, other articles which are adequately secured or by an appropriate blocking or immobilization method, it must be secured by at least one tiedown for every 3.04 meters (10 feet) of article length, or fraction thereof.

(d) Special rule for special purpose vehicles. The rules in this section do not apply to a vehicle transporting one or more articles of cargo such as, but not limited to, machinery or fabricated structural items (e.g., steel or concrete beams, crane booms, girders, and trusses, etc.) which, because of their design, size, shape, or weight, must be fastened by special methods. However, any article of cargo carried on that vehicle must be securely and adequately fastened to the vehicle.

§393.112 Must a tiedown be adjustable?

Each tiedown, or its associated connectors, or its attachment mechanisms must be designed, constructed, and maintained so the driver of an in-transit commercial motor vehicle can tighten them. However, this requirement does not apply to the use of steel strapping.

§393.114 What are the requirements for front end structures used as part of a cargo securement system?

(a) **Applicability.** The rules in this section are applicable to commercial motor vehicles transporting articles of cargo that are in contact with the front end structure of the vehicle. The front end structure on these cargo-carrying vehicles must meet the performance requirements of this section.

(b) **Height and width.** (1) The front end structure must extend either to a height of 4 feet above the floor of the vehicle or to a height at which it blocks forward movement of any item or article of cargo being carried on the vehicle, whichever is lower.

(2) The front end structure must have a width which is at least equal to the width of the vehicle or which blocks forward movement of any article of cargo being transported on the vehicle, whichever is narrower.

(c) **Strength.** The front end structure must be capable of withstanding the following horizontal forward static load:

(1) For a front end structure less than 6 feet in height, a horizontal forward static load equal to one-half (0.5) of the weight of the articles of cargo being transported on the vehicle uniformly distributed over the entire portion of the front end structure that is within 4 feet above the vehicle's floor or that is at or below a height above the vehicle's floor at which it blocks forward movement of any article of the vehicle's cargo, whichever is less; or

(2) For a front end structure 6 feet in height or higher, a horizontal forward static load equal to four-tenths (0.4) of the weight of the articles of cargo being transported on the vehicle uniformly distributed over the entire front end structure.

(d) **Penetration resistance.** The front end structure must be designed, constructed, and maintained so that it is capable of resisting penetration by any article of cargo that contacts it when the vehicle decelerates at a rate of 20 feet per second,

4.3 Cargo Securement Regulations

per second. The front end structure must have no aperture large enough to permit any article of cargo in contact with the structure to pass through it.

(e) **Substitute devices.** The requirements of this section may be met by the use of devices performing the same functions as a front end structure, if the devices are at least as strong as, and provide protection against shifting articles of cargo at least equal to, a front end structure which conforms to those requirements.

Specific Securement Requirements by Commodity Type

§393.116 What are the rules for securing logs?

(a) **Applicability.** The rules in this section are applicable to the transportation of logs with the following exceptions:

(1) Logs that are unitized by banding or other comparable means may be transported in accordance with the general cargo securement rules of §§393.100 through 393.114.

(2) Loads that consist of no more than four processed logs may be transported in accordance with the general cargo securement rules of §§393.100 through 393.114.

(3) Firewood, stumps, log debris and other such short logs must be transported in a vehicle or container enclosed on both sides, front, and rear and of adequate strength to contain them. Longer logs may also be so loaded.

(b) **Components of a securement system.** (1) Logs must be transported on a vehicle designed and built, or adapted, for the transportation of logs. Any such vehicle must be fitted with bunks, bolsters, stakes or standards, or other equivalent means, that cradle the logs and prevent them from rolling.

(2) All vehicle components involved in securement of logs must be designed and built to withstand all anticipated operational forces without failure, accidental release or permanent deformation. Stakes or standards that are not permanently attached to the vehicle must be secured in a manner that prevents unintentional separation from the vehicle in transit.

(3) Tiedowns must be used in combination with the stabilization provided by bunks, stakes, and bolsters to secure the load unless the logs:

(i) are transported in a crib-type log trailer (as defined in 49 CFR 393.5), and

(ii) are loaded in compliance with paragraphs (b)(2) and (c) of this section.

(4) The aggregate working load limit for tiedowns used to secure a stack of logs on a frame vehicle, or a flatbed vehicle equipped with bunks, bolsters, or stakes must be at least on-sixth the weight of the stack of logs.

(c) **Use of securement system.** (1) Logs must be solidly packed, and the outer bottom logs must be in contact with and resting solidly against the bunks, bolsters, stakes or standards.

(2) Each outside log on the side of a stack of logs must touch at least two stakes, bunks, bolsters, or standards. If one end does not actually touch a stake, it must rest on other logs in a

4.3 Cargo Securement Regulations

stable manner and must extend beyond the stake, bunk, bolster or standard.

(3) The center of the highest outside log on each side or end must be below the top of each stake, bunk or standard.

(4) Each log that is not held in place by contact with other logs or the stakes, bunks, or standards must be held in place by a tiedown. Additional tiedowns or securement devices must be used when the condition of the wood results in such low friction between logs that they are likely to slip upon each other.

(d) **Securement of shortwood logs loaded crosswise on frame, rail and flatbed vehicles.** In addition to the requirements of paragraphs (b) and (c) of this section, each stack of logs loaded crosswise must meet the following rules:

(1) In no case may the end of a log in the lower tier extend more than one-third of the log's total length beyond the nearest supporting structure on the vehicle.

(2) When only one stack of shortwood is loaded crosswise, it must be secured with at least two tiedowns. The tiedowns must attach to the vehicle frame at the front and rear of the load, and must cross the load in this direction.

(3) When two tiedowns are used, they must be positioned at approximately one-third and two-thirds of the length of the logs.

(4) A vehicle that is more than 10 meters (33 feet) long must be equipped with center stakes, or comparable devices, to divide it into sections approximately equal in length. Where a vehicle is so divided, each tiedown must secure the highest log on each side of the center stake, and must be fastened below these logs. It may be fixed at each end and tensioned from the middle, or fixed in the middle and tensioned from each end, or it may pass through a pulley or equivalent device in the middle and be tensioned from one end.

(5) Any structure or stake that is subjected to an upward force when the tiedowns are tensioned must be anchored to resist that force.

(6) If two stacks of shortwood are loaded side-by-side, in addition to meeting the requirements of paragraphs (d)(1) through (d)(5) of this section, they must be loaded so that:

(i) There is no space between the two stacks of logs;

(ii) The outside of each stack is raised at least 2.5 cm (1 in) within 10 cm (4 in) of the end of the logs or the side of the vehicle;

(iii) The highest log is no more than 2.44 m (8 ft) above the deck; and

(iv) At least one tiedown is used lengthwise across each stack of logs.

(e) **Securement of logs loaded lengthwise on flatbed and frame vehicles.** (1) Shortwood. In addition to meeting the requirements of paragraphs (b) and (c) of this section, each stack of shortwood loaded lengthwise on a frame vehicle or

4.3 Cargo Securement Regulations

on a flatbed must be cradled in a bunk unit or contained by stakes and

(i) Secured to the vehicle by at least two tiedowns, or

(ii) If all the logs in any stack are blocked in the front by a front-end structure strong enough to restrain the load, or by another stack of logs, and blocked in the rear by another stack of logs or vehicle end structure, the stack may be secured with one tiedown. If one tiedown is used, it must be positioned about midway between the stakes, or

(iii) Be bound by at least two tiedown-type devices such as wire rope, used as wrappers that encircle the entire load at locations along the load that provide effective securement. If wrappers are being used to bundle the logs together, the wrappers are not required to be attached to the vehicle.

(2) Longwood. Longwood must be cradled in two or more bunks and must either:

(i) Be secured to the vehicle by at least two tiedowns at locations that provide effective securement, or

(ii) Be bound by at least two tiedown-type devices, such as wire rope, used as wrappers that encircle the entire load at locations along the load that provide effective securement. If a wrapper(s) is being used to bundle the logs together, the wrapper is not required to be attached to the vehicle.

(f) **Securement of logs transported on pole trailers.** (1) The load must be secured by at least one tiedown at each bunk, or alternatively, by at least two tiedowns used as wrappers that encircle the entire load at locations along the load that provide effective securement.

(2) The front and rear wrappers must be at least 3.04 meters (10 feet) apart.

(3) Large diameter single and double log loads must be immobilized with chock blocks or other equivalent means to prevent shifting.

(4) Large diameter logs that rise above bunks must be secured to the underlying load with at least two additional wrappers.

§393.118 What are the rules for securing dressed lumber or similar building products?

(a) **Applicability.** The rules in this section apply to the transportation of bundles of dressed lumber, packaged lumber, building products such as plywood, gypsum board or other materials of similar shape. Lumber or building products which are not bundled or packaged must be treated as loose items and transported in accordance with §§393.100 through 393.114 of this subpart. For the purpose of this section, "bundle" refers to packages of lumber, building materials or similar products which are unitized for securement as a single article of cargo.

(b) **Positioning of bundles.** Bundles must be placed side by side in direct contact with each other, or a means must be provided to prevent bundles from shifting towards each other.

4.3 Cargo Securement Regulations

(c) **Securement of bundles transported using no more than one tier.** Bundles carried on one tier must be secured in accordance with the general provisions of §§393.100 through 393.114.

(d) **Securement of bundles transported using more than one tier.** Bundles carried in more than one tier must be either:

(1) Blocked against lateral movement by stakes on the sides of the vehicle and secured by tiedowns laid out over the top tier, as outlined in the general provisions of §§393.100 through 393.114; or

(2) Restrained from lateral movement by blocking or high friction devices between tiers and secured by tiedowns laid out over the top tier, as outlined in the general provisions of §§393.100 through 393.114; or

(3) Placed directly on top of other bundles or on spacers and secured in accordance with the following:

(i) The length of spacers between bundles must provide support to all pieces in the bottom row of the bundle.

(ii) The width of individual spacers must be equal to or greater than the height.

(iii) If spacers are comprised of layers of material, the layers must be unitized or fastened together in a manner which ensures that the spacer performs as a single piece of material.

(iv) The arrangement of the tiedowns for the bundles must be:

(A) Secured by tiedowns over the top tier of bundles, in accordance with the general provisions of §§393.100 through 393.114 with a minimum of two tiedowns for bundles longer than 1.52 meters (5 ft); and

(B) Secured by tiedowns as follows:

(1) If there are 3 tiers, the middle and top bundles must be secured by tiedowns in accordance with the general provisions of §§393.100 through 393.114; or

(2)(i) If there are more than 3 tiers, then one of the middle bundles and the top bundle must be secured by tiedown devices in accordance with the general provision of §§393.100 through 393.114, and the maximum height for the middle tier that must be secured may not exceed 6 feet about the deck of the trailer; or

(ii) Otherwise, the second tier from the bottom must be secured in accordance with the general provisions of §§393.100 through 393.114; or

(4) Secured by tiedowns over each tier of bundles, in accordance with §§393.100 through 393.114 using a minimum of two tiedowns over each of the top bundles longer than 1.52 meters (5 ft), in all circumstances; or

(5) When loaded in a sided vehicle or container of adequate strength, dressed lumber or similar building products may be secured in accordance with the general provisions of §§393.100 through 393.114.

4.3 Cargo Securement Regulations

§393.120 What are the rules for securing metal coils?

(a) **Applicability.** The rules in this section apply to the transportation of one or more metal coils which, individually or grouped together, weigh 2268 kg (5000 pounds) or more. Shipments of metal coils that weigh less than 2268 kg (5000 pounds) may be secured in accordance with the provisions of §§393.100 through 393.114.

(b) **Securement of coils transported with eyes vertical on a flatbed vehicle, in a sided vehicle or intermodal container with anchor points**—(1) An individual coil. Each coil must be secured by tiedowns arranged in a manner to prevent the coils from tipping in the forward, rearward, and lateral directions. The restraint system must include the following:

(i) At least one tiedown attached diagonally from the left side of the vehicle or intermodal container (near the forwardmost part of the coil), across the eye of the coil, to the right side of the vehicle or intermodal container (near the rearmost part of the coil);

(ii) At least one tiedown attached diagonally from the right side of the vehicle or intermodal container (near the forwardmost part of the coil), across the eye of the coil, to the left side of the vehicle or intermodal container (near the rearmost part of the coil);

(iii) At least one tiedown attached transversely over the eye of the coil; and

(iv) Either blocking and bracing, friction mats or tiedowns must be used to prevent longitudinal movement in the forward direction.

(2) Coils grouped in rows. When coils are grouped and loaded side by side in a transverse or longitudinal row, the each row of coils must be secured by the following:

(i) At least one tiedown attached to the front of the row of coils, restraining against forward motion, and whenever practicable, making an angle no more than 45 degrees with the floor of the vehicle or intermodal container when viewed from the side of the vehicle or container;

(ii) At least one tiedown attached to the rear of the row of coils, restraining against rearward motion, and whenever practicable, making an angle no more than 45 degrees with the floor of the vehicle or intermodal container when viewed from the side of the vehicle or container;

(iii) At least one tiedown over the top of each coil or transverse row of coils, restraining against vertical motion. Tiedowns going over the top of a coil(s) must be as close as practicable to the eye of the coil and positioned to prevent the tiedown from slipping or becoming unintentionally unfastened while the vehicle is in transit; and

(iv) Tiedowns must be arranged to prevent shifting or tipping in the forward, rearward and lateral directions.

(c) **Securement of coils transported with eyes crosswise on a flatbed vehicle, in a sided vehicle or intermodal con-**

4.3 Cargo Securement Regulations

tainer with anchor points–(1) An individual coil. Each coil must be secured by the following:

(i) A means (*e.g.*, timbers, chocks or wedges, a cradle, etc.) to prevent the coil from rolling. The means of preventing rolling must support the coil off the deck, and must not be capable of becoming unintentionally unfastened or loose while the vehicle is in transit. If timbers, chocks or wedges are used, they must be held in place by coil bunks or similar devices to prevent them from coming loose. The use of nailed blocking or cleats as the sole means to secure timbers, chocks or wedges, or a nailed wood cradle, is prohibited;

(ii) At least one tiedown through its eye, restricting against forward motion, and whenever practicable, making an angle no more than 45 degrees with the floor of the vehicle or intermodal container when viewed from the side of the vehicle or container; and

(iii) At least one tiedown through its eye, restricting against rearward motion, and whenever practicable, making an angle no more than 45 degrees with the floor of the vehicle or intermodal container when viewed from the side of the vehicle or container.

(2) Prohibition on crossing of tiedowns when coils are transported with eyes crosswise. Attaching tiedowns diagonally through the eye of a coil to form an X-pattern when viewed from above the vehicle is prohibited.

(d) **Securement of coils transported with eyes lengthwise on a flatbed vehicle, in a sided vehicle or intermodal con-**

tainer with anchor points–(1) An individual coil-option 1. Each coil must be secured by:

(i) A means (*e.g.*, timbers, chocks or wedges, a cradle, etc.) to prevent the coil from rolling. The means of preventing rolling must support the coil off the deck, and must not be capable of becoming unintentionally unfastened or loose while the vehicle is in transit. If timbers, chocks or wedges are used, they must be held in place by coil bunks or similar devices to prevent them from coming loose. The use of nailed blocking or cleats as the sole means to secure timbers, chocks or wedges, or a nailed wood cradle, is prohibited;

(ii) At least one tiedown attached diagonally through its eye from the left side of the vehicle or intermodal container (near the forward- most part of the coil), to the right side of the vehicle or intermodal container (near the rearmost part of the coil), making an angle no more than 45 degrees, whenever practicable, with the floor of the vehicle or intermodal container when viewed from the side of the vehicle or container;

(iii) At least one tiedown attached diagonally through its eye, from the right side of the vehicle or intermodal container (near the forward-most part of the coil), to the left side of the vehicle or intermodal container (near the rearmost part of the coil), making an angle no more than 45 degrees, whenever practicable, with the floor of the vehicle or intermodal container when viewed from the side of the vehicle or container;

(iv) At least one tiedown attached transversely over the top of the coil; and

4.3 Cargo Securement Regulations

(v) Either blocking, or friction mats to prevent longitudinal movement.

(2) An individual coil-option 2. Each coil must be secured by:

(i) A means (*e.g.*, timbers, chocks or wedges, a cradle, etc.) to prevent the coil from rolling. The means of preventing rolling must support the coil off the deck, and must not be capable of becoming unintentionally unfastened or loose while the vehicle is in transit. If timbers, chocks or wedges are used, they must be held in place by coil bunks or similar devices to prevent them from coming loose. The use of nailed blocking or cleats as the sole means to secure timbers, chocks or wedges, or a nailed wood cradle, is prohibited;

(ii) At least one tiedown attached straight through its eye from the left side of the vehicle or intermodal container (near the forward- most part of the coil), to the left side of the vehicle or intermodal container (near the rearmost part of the coil), and, whenever practicable, making an angle no more than 45 degrees with the floor of the vehicle or intermodal container when viewed from the side of the vehicle or container;

(iii) At least one tiedown attached straight through its eye, from the right side of the vehicle or intermodal container (near the forward-most part of the coil), to the right side of the vehicle or intermodal container (near the rearmost part of the coil), and whenever practicable, making an angle no more than 45 degrees with the floor of the vehicle or intermodal container when viewed from the side of the vehicle or container;

(iv) At least one tiedown attached transversely over the top of the coil; and

(v) Either blocking or friction mats to prevent longitudinal movement.

(3) An individual coil-option 3. Each coil must be secured by:

(i) A means (*e.g.*, timbers, chocks or wedges, a cradle, etc.) to prevent the coil from rolling. The means of preventing rolling must support the coil off the deck, and must not be capable of becoming unintentionally unfastened or loose while the vehicle is in transit. If timbers, chocks or wedges are used, they must be held in place by coil bunks or similar devices to prevent them from coming loose. The use of nailed blocking or cleats as the sole means to secure timbers, chocks or wedges, or a nailed wood cradle, is prohibited;

(ii) At least one tiedown over the top of the coil, located near the forward-most part of the coil;

(iii) At least one tiedown over the top of the coil located near the rearmost part of the coil; and

(iv) Either blocking or friction mats to prevent longitudinal movement.he forward direction.

(4) Rows of coils. Each transverse row of coils having approximately equal outside diameters must be secured with:

(i) A means (*e.g.*, timbers, chocks or wedges, a cradle, etc.) to prevent each coil in the row of coils from rolling. The means of preventing rolling must support each coil off the deck, and must not be capable of becoming unintentionally

4.3 Cargo Securement Regulations

unfastened or loose while the vehicle is in transit. If timbers, chocks or wedges are used, they must be held in place by coil bunks or similar devices to prevent them from coming loose. The use of nailed blocking or cleats as the sole means to secure timbers, chocks or wedges, or a nailed wood cradle, is prohibited;

(ii) At least one tiedown over the top of each coil or transverse row, located near the forward-most part of the coil;

(iii) At least one tiedown over the top of each coil or transverse row, located near the rearmost part of the coil; and

(iv) Either blocking, bracing or friction mats to prevent longitudinal movement.

(e) **Securement of coils transported in a sided vehicle without anchor points or an intermodal container without anchor points.** Metal coils transported in a vehicle with sides without anchor points or an intermodal container without anchor points must be loaded in a manner to prevent shifting and tipping. The coils may also be secured using a system of blocking and bracing, friction mats, tiedowns, or a combination of these to prevent any horizontal movement and tipping.

§393.122 What are the rules for securing paper rolls?

(a) **Applicability.** The rules in this section apply to shipments of paper rolls which, individually or together, weigh 2268 kg (5000 lb) or more. Shipments of paper rolls that weigh less than 2268 kg (5000 lb), and paper rolls that are unitized on a pallet, may either be secured in accordance with the rules in this section or the requirements of §§393.100 through 393.114.

(b) **Securement of paper rolls transported with eyes vertical in a sided vehicle.** (1) Paper rolls must be placed tightly against the walls of the vehicle, other paper rolls, or other cargo, to prevent movement during transit.

(2) If there are not enough paper rolls in the shipment to reach the walls of the vehicle, lateral movement must be prevented by filling the void, blocking, bracing, tiedowns or friction mats. The paper rolls may also be banded together.

(3) When any void behind a group of paper rolls, including that at the rear of the vehicle, exceeds the diameter of the paper rolls, rearward movement must be prevented by friction mats, blocking, bracing, tiedowns, or banding to other rolls.

(4)(i) If a paper roll is not prevented from tipping or falling sideways or rearwards by vehicle structure or other cargo, and its width is more than 2 times its diameter, it must be prevented from tipping or falling by banding it to other rolls, bracing, or tiedowns.

(ii) If the forwardmost roll(s) in a group of paper rolls has a width greater than 1.75 times its diameter and it is not prevented from tipping or falling forwards by vehicle structure or other cargo, then it must be prevented from tipping or falling forwards by banding it to other rolls, bracing, or tiedowns.

(iii) If the forwardmost roll(s) in a group of paper rolls has a width equal to or less than 1.75 times its diameter, and it is

4.3 Cargo Securement Regulations

restrained against forward movement by friction mat(s) alone, then banding, bracing, or tiedowns are not required to prevent tipping or falling forwards.

(iv) If a paper roll or the forwardmost roll in a group of paper rolls has a width greater than 1.25 times its diameter, and it is not prevented from tipping or falling forwards by vehicle structure or other cargo, and it is not restrained against forward movement by friction mat(s) alone, then it must be prevented from tipping or falling by banding it to other rolls, bracing or tiedowns.

(5) If paper rolls are banded together, the rolls must be placed tightly against each other to form a stable group. The bands must be applied tightly, and must be secured so that they cannot fall off the rolls or to the deck.

(6) A friction mat used to provide the principal securement for a paper roll must protrude from beneath the roll in the direction in which it is providing that securement.

(c) **Securement of split loads of paper rolls transported with eyes vertical in a sided vehicle.** (1) If a paper roll in a split load is not prevented from forward movement by vehicle structure or other cargo, it must be prevented from forward movement by filling the open space, or by blocking, bracing, tiedowns, friction mats, or some combination of these.

(2) A friction mat used to provide the principal securement for a paper roll must protrude from beneath the roll in the direction in which it is providing that securement.

(d) **Securement of stacked loads of paper rolls transported with eyes vertical in a sided vehicle.** (1) Paper rolls must not be loaded on a layer of paper rolls beneath unless the lower layer extends to the front of the vehicle.

(2) Paper rolls in the second and subsequent layers must be prevented from forward, rearward or lateral movement by means as allowed for the bottom layer, or by use of a blocking roll from a lower layer.

(3) The blocking roll must be at least 38 mm (1.5 in) taller than other rolls, or must be raised at least 38 mm (1.5 in) using dunnage.

(4) A roll in the rearmost row of any layer raised using dunnage may not be secured by friction mats alone.

(e) **Securement of paper rolls transported with eyes crosswise in a sided vehicle.** (1) The paper rolls must be prevented from rolling or shifting longitudinally by contact with vehicle structure or other cargo, by chocks, wedges or blocking and bracing of adequate size, or by tiedowns.

(2) Chocks, wedges or blocking must be held securely in place by some means in addition to friction, so they cannot become unintentionally unfastened or loose while the vehicle is in transit.

(3) The rearmost roll must not be secured using the rear doors of the vehicle or intermodal container, or by blocking held in place by those doors.

4.3 Cargo Securement Regulations

(4) If there is more than a total of 203 mm (8 in) of space between the ends of a paper roll, or a row of rolls, and the walls of the vehicle, void fillers, blocking, bracing, friction mats, or tiedowns must be used to prevent the roll from shifting towards either wall.

(f) **Securement of stacked loads of paper rolls transported with eyes crosswise in a sided vehicle.** (1) Rolls must not be loaded in a second layer unless the bottom layer extends to the front of the vehicle.

(2) Rolls must not be loaded in a third or higher layer unless all wells in the layer beneath are filled.

(3) The foremost roll in each upper layer, or any roll with an empty well in front of it, must be secured against forward movement by:

(i) Banding it to other rolls, or

(ii) Blocking against an adequately secured eye-vertical blocking roll resting on the floor of the vehicle which is at least 1.5 times taller than the diameter of the roll being blocked, or

(iii) Placing it in a well formed by two rolls on the lower row whose diameter is equal to or greater than that of the roll on the upper row.

(4) The rearmost roll in each upper layer must be secured by banding it to other rolls if it is located in either of the last two wells formed by the rearmost rolls in the layer below.

(5) Rolls must be secured against lateral movement by the same means allowed for the bottom layer when there is more than a total of 203 mm (8 in) of space between the ends of a paper roll, or a row of rolls, and the walls of the vehicle.

(g) **Securement of paper rolls transported with the eyes lengthwise in a sided vehicle.**

(1) Each roll must be prevented from forward movement by contact with vehicle structure, other cargo, blocking or tiedowns.

(2) Each roll must be prevented from rearward movement by contact with other cargo, blocking, friction mats or tiedowns.

(3) The paper rolls must be prevented from rolling or shifting laterally by contact with the wall of the vehicle or other cargo, or by chocks, wedges or blocking of adequate size.

(4) Chocks, wedges or blocking must be held securely in place by some means in addition to friction, so they cannot become unintentionally unfastened or loose while the vehicle is in transit.

(h) **Securement of stacked loads of paper rolls transported with the eyes lengthwise in a sided vehicle.** (1) Rolls must not be loaded in a higher layer if another roll will fit in the layer beneath.

(2) An upper layer must be formed by placing paper rolls in the wells formed by the rolls beneath.

(3) A roll in an upper layer must be secured against forward and rearward movement by any of the means allowed for the bottom layer, by use of a blocking roll, or by banding to other rolls.

4.3 Cargo Securement Regulations

(i) **Securement of paper rolls transported on a flatbed vehicle or in a curtain-sided vehicle**–(1) Paper rolls with eyes vertical or with eyes lengthwise.

(i) The paper rolls must be loaded and secured as described for a sided vehicle, and the entire load must be secured by tiedowns in accordance with the requirements of §§393.100 through 393.114.

(ii) Stacked loads of paper rolls with eyes vertical are prohibited.

(2) Paper rolls with eyes crosswise. (i) The paper rolls must be prevented from rolling or shifting longitudinally by contact with vehicle structure or other cargo, by chocks, wedges or blocking and bracing of adequate size, or by tiedowns.

(ii) Chocks, wedges or blocking must be held securely in place by some means in addition to friction so that they cannot become unintentionally unfastened or loose while the vehicle is in transit.

(iii) Tiedowns must be used in accordance with the requirements of §§393.100 through 393.114 to prevent lateral movement.

§393.124 What are the rules for securing concrete pipe?

(a) **Applicability.** (1) The rules in this section apply to the transportation of concrete pipe on flatbed trailers and vehicles, and lowboy trailers.

(2) Concrete pipe bundled tightly together into a single rigid article that has no tendency to roll, and concrete pipe loaded in a sided vehicle or container must be secured in accordance with the provisions of §§393.100 through 393.114.

(b) **General specifications for tiedowns.** (1) The aggregate working load limit of all tiedowns on any group of pipes must not be less than half the total weight of all the pipes in the group.

(2) A transverse tiedown through a pipe on an upper tier or over longitudinal tiedowns is considered to secure all those pipes beneath on which that tiedown causes pressure.

(c) **Blocking.** (1) Blocking may be one or more pieces placed symmetrically about the center of a pipe.

(2) One piece must extend at least half the distance from the center to each end of the pipe, and two pieces must be placed on the opposite side, one at each end of the pipe.

(3) Blocking must be placed firmly against the pipe, and must be secured to prevent it moving out from under the pipe.

(4) Timber blocking must have minimum dimensions of at least 10 x 15 cm (4 x 6 in).

(d) **Arranging the load**–(1) *Pipe of different diameter.* If pipe of more than one diameter are loaded on a vehicle, groups must be formed that consist of pipe of only one size, and each group must be separately secured.

(2) *Arranging a bottom tier.* The bottom tier must be arranged to cover the full length of the vehicle, or as a partial tier in one group or two groups.

4.3 Cargo Securement Regulations

(3) *Arranging an upper tier.* Pipe must be placed only in the wells formed by adjacent pipes in the tier beneath. A third or higher tier must not be started unless all wells in the tier beneath are filled.

(4) *Arranging the top tier.* The top tier must be arranged as a complete tier, a partial tier in one group, or a partial tier in two groups.

(5) *Arranging bell pipe.* (i) Bell pipe must be loaded on at least two longitudinal spacers of sufficient height to ensure that the bell is clear of the deck.

(ii) Bell pipe loaded in one tier must have the bells alternating on opposite sides of the vehicle.

(iii) The ends of consecutive pipe must be staggered, if possible, within the allowable width, otherwise they must be aligned.

(iv) Bell pipe loaded in more than one tier must have the bells of the bottom tier all on the same side of the vehicle.

(v) Pipe in every upper tier must be loaded with bells on the opposite side of the vehicle to the bells of the tier below.

(vi) If the second tier is not complete, pipe in the bottom tier which do not support a pipe above must have their bells alternating on opposite sides of the vehicle.

(e) **Securing pipe with an inside diameter up to 1,143 mm (45 in).** In addition to the requirements of paragraphs (b), (c) and (d) of this section, the following rules must be satisfied:

(1) *Stabilizing the bottom tier.* (i) The bottom tier must be immobilized longitudinally at each end by blocking, vehicle end structure, stakes, a locked pipe unloader, or other equivalent means.

(ii) Other pipe in the bottom tier may also be held in place by blocks and/or wedges; and

(iii) Every pipe in the bottom tier must also be held firmly in contact with the adjacent pipe by tiedowns though the front and rear pipes:

(A) At least one tiedown through the front pipe of the bottom tier must run aft at an angle not more than 45 degrees with the horizontal, whenever practicable.

(B) At least one tiedown through the rear pipe of the bottom tier must run forward at an angle not more than 45 degrees with the horizontal, whenever practicable.

(2) *Use of tiedowns.* (i) Each pipe may be secured individually with tiedowns through the pipe.

(ii) If each pipe is not secured individually with a tiedown, then:

(A) Either one 1/2-inch diameter chain or wire rope, or two 3/8-inch diameter chain or wire rope, must be placed longitudinally over the group of pipes;

(B) One transverse tiedown must be used for every 3.04 m (10 ft) of load length. The transverse tiedowns may be placed through a pipe, or over both longitudinal tiedowns between two pipes on the top tier.

4.3 Cargo Securement Regulations

(C) If the first pipe of a group in the top tier is not placed in the first well formed by pipes at the front of the tier beneath, it must be secured by an additional tiedown that runs rearward at an angle not more than 45 degrees to the horizontal, whenever practicable. This tiedown must pass either through the front pipe of the upper tier, or outside it and over both longitudinal tiedowns; and

(D) If the last pipe of a group in the top tier is not placed in the last well formed by pipes at the rear of the tier beneath, it must be secured by an additional tiedown that runs forward at an angle not more than 45 degrees to the horizontal, whenever practicable. This tiedown must pass either through the rear pipe of the upper tier or outside it and over both longitudinal tiedowns.

(f) **Securing large pipe, with an inside diameter over 1143 mm (45 in).** In addition to the requirements of paragraphs (b), (c) and (d) of this section, the following rules must be satisfied:

(1) The front pipe and the rear pipe must be immobilized by blocking, wedges, vehicle end structure, stakes, locked pipe unloader, or other equivalent means.

(2) Each pipe must be secured by tiedowns through the pipe:

(i) At least one tiedown through each pipe in the front half of the load, which includes the middle one if there is an odd number, and must run rearward at an angle not more than 45 degrees with the horizontal, whenever practicable.

(ii) At least one tiedown through each pipe in the rear half of the load, and must run forward at an angle not more than 45 degrees with the horizontal, whenever practicable, to hold each pipe firmly in contact with adjacent pipe; and

(iii) If the front or rear pipe is not also in contact with vehicle end structure, stakes, a locked pipe unloader, or other equivalent means, at least two tiedowns positioned as described in paragraphs (f)(2)(i) and (ii) of this section, must be used through that pipe.

(3) If only one pipe is transported, or if several pipes are transported without contact between other pipes, the requirements in this paragraph apply to each pipe as a single front and rear article.

§393.126 What are the rules for securing intermodal containers?

(a) **Applicability.** The rules in this section apply to the transportation of intermodal containers. Cargo contained within an intermodal container must be secured in accordance with the provisions of §§393.100 through 393.114 or, if applicable, the commodity specific rules of this part.

(b) **Securement of intermodal containers transported on container chassis vehicle(s).** (1) All lower corners of the intermodal container must be secured to the container chassis with securement devices or integral locking devices that cannot unintentionally become unfastened while the vehicle is in transit.

4.3 Cargo Securement Regulations

(2) The securement devices must restrain the container from moving more than 1.27 cm (1/2 in) forward, more than 1.27 cm (1/2 in) aft, more than 1.27 cm (1/2 in) to the right, more than 1.27 cm (1/2 in) to the left, or more than 2.54 cm (1 in) vertically.

(3) The front and rear of the container must be secured independently.

(c) **Securement of loaded intermodal containers transported on vehicles other than container chassis vehicle(s).** (1) All lower corners of the intermodal container must rest upon the vehicle, or the corners must be supported by a structure capable of bearing the weight of the container and that support structure must be independently secured to the motor vehicle.

(2) Each container must be secured to the vehicle by:

(i) Chains, wire ropes or integral devices which are fixed to all lower corners; or

(ii) Crossed chains which are fixed to all upper corners; and,

(3) The front and rear of the container must be secured independently. Each chain, wire rope, or integral locking device must be attached to the container in a manner that prevents it from being unintentionally unfastened while the vehicle is in transit.

(d) **Securement of empty intermodal containers transported on vehicles other than container chassis vehicle(s).** Empty intermodal containers transported on vehicles other than container chassis vehicles do not have to have all lower corners of the intermodal container resting upon the vehicle, or have all lower corners supported by a structure capable of bearing the weight of the empty container, provided:

(1) The empty intermodal container is balanced and positioned on the vehicle in a manner such that the container is stable before the addition of tiedowns or other securement equipment;

(2) The amount of overhang for the empty container on the trailer does not exceed five feet on either the front or rear of the trailer;

(3) The empty intermodal container must not interfere with the vehicle's maneuverability; and,

(4) The empty intermodal container is secured to prevent lateral, longitudinal, or vertical shifting.

§393.128 What are the rules for securing automobiles, light trucks and vans?

(a) **Applicability.** The rules in this section apply to the transportation of automobiles, light trucks, and vans which individually weigh 4,536 kg. (10,000 lb) or less. Vehicles which individually are heavier than 4,536 kg (10,000 lb) must be secured in accordance with the provisions of §393.130 of this part.

(b) **Securement of automobiles, light trucks, and vans.**

4.3 Cargo Securement Regulations

(1) Automobiles, light trucks, and vans must be restrained at both the front and rear to prevent lateral, forward, rearward, and vertical movement using a minimum of two tiedowns.

(2) Tiedowns that are designed to be affixed to the structure of the automobile, light truck, or van must use the mounting points on those vehicles that have been specifically designed for that purpose.

(3) Tiedowns that are designed to fit over or around the wheels of an automobile, light truck, or van must provide restraint in the lateral, longitudinal and vertical directions.

(4) Edge protectors are not required for synthetic webbing at points where the webbing comes in contact with the tires.

§393.130 What are the rules for securing heavy vehicles, equipment and machinery?

(a) **Applicability.** The rules in this section apply to the transportation of heavy vehicles, equipment and machinery which operate on wheels or tracks, such as front end loaders, bulldozers, tractors, and power shovels and which individually weigh 4,536 kg (10,000 lb.) or more. Vehicles, equipment and machinery which is lighter than 4,536 kg (10,000 lb.) may also be secured in accordance with the provisions of this section, with §393.128, or in accordance with the provisions of §§393.100 through 393.114.

(b) **Preparation of equipment being transported.** (1) Accessory equipment, such as hydraulic shovels, must be completely lowered and secured to the vehicle.

(2) Articulated vehicles shall be restrained in a manner that prevents articulation while in transit.

(c) **Securement of heavy vehicles, equipment or machinery with crawler tracks or wheels.** (1) In addition to the requirements of paragraph (b) of this section, heavy equipment or machinery with crawler tracks or wheels must be restrained against movement in the lateral, forward, rearward, and vertical direction using a minimum of four tiedowns.

(2) Each of the tiedowns must be affixed as close as practicable to the front and rear of the vehicle, or mounting points on the vehicle that have been specifically designed for that purpose.

§393.132 What are the rules for securing flattened or crushed vehicles?

(a) **Applicability.** The rules in this section apply to the transportation of vehicles such as automobiles, light trucks, and vans that have been flattened or crushed.

(b) **Prohibition on the use of synthetic webbing.** The use of synthetic webbing to secure flattened or crushed vehicles is prohibited except that such webbing may be used to connect wire rope or chain to anchor points on the commercial motor vehicle. However, the webbing (regardless of whether edge protection is used) must not come into contact with the flattened or crushed cars.

4.3 Cargo Securement Regulations

(c) **Securement of flattened or crushed vehicles.** Flattened or crushed vehicles must be transported on vehicles which have:

(1) Containment walls or comparable means on four sides which extend to the full height of the load and which block against movement of the cargo in the forward, rearward and lateral directions; or

(2)(i) Containment walls or comparable means on three sides which extend to the full height of the load and which block against movement of the cargo in the direction for which there is a containment wall or comparable means, and

(ii) A minimum of two tiedowns are required per vehicle stack; or

(3)(i) Containment walls on two sides which extend to the full height of the load and which block against movement of the cargo in the forward and rearward directions, and

(ii) A minimum of three tiedowns are required per vehicle stack; or

(4) A minimum of four tiedowns per vehicle stack.

(5) In addition to the requirements of paragraphs (c)(2), (3), and (4), the following rules must be satisfied:

(i) Vehicles used to transport flattened or crushed vehicles must be equipped with a means to prevent liquids from leaking from the bottom of the vehicle, and loose parts from falling from the bottom and all four sides of the vehicle extending to the full height of the cargo.

(ii) The means used to contain loose parts may consist of structural walls, sides or sideboards, or suitable covering material, alone or in combinations.

(iii) The use of synthetic material for containment of loose parts is permitted.

§393.134 What are the rules for securing roll-on/roll-off or hook lift containers?

(a) **Applicability.** The rules in this section apply to the transportation of roll-on/roll-off or hook lift containers.

(b) **Securement of a roll-on/roll-off and hook lift container.** Each roll-on/roll-off and hook lift container carried on a vehicle which is not equipped with an integral securement system must be:

(1) Blocked against forward movement by the lifting device, stops, a combination of both or other suitable restraint mechanism;

(2) Secured to the front of the vehicle by the lifting device or other suitable restraint against lateral and vertical movement;

(3) Secured to the rear of the vehicle with at least one of the following mechanisms:

(i) One tiedown attached to both the vehicle chassis and the container chassis;

(ii) Two tiedowns installed lengthwise, each securing one side of the container to one of the vehicle's side rails; or

4.3 Cargo Securement Regulations

(iii) Two hooks, or an equivalent mechanism, securing both sides of the container to the vehicle chassis at least as effectively as the tiedowns in the two previous items.

(4) The mechanisms used to secure the rear end of a roll-on/roll off or hook lift container must be installed no more than two meters (6 ft 7 in) from the rear of the container.

(5) In the event that one or more of the front stops or lifting devices are missing, damaged or not compatible, additional manually installed tiedowns must be used to secure the container to the vehicle, providing the same level of securement as the missing, damaged or incompatible components.

§393.136 What are the rules for securing large boulders?

(a) **Applicability.** (1) The rules in this section are applicable to the transportation of any large piece of natural, irregularly shaped rock weighing in excess of 5,000 kg (11,000 lb.) or with a volume in excess of 2 cubic-meters on an open vehicle, or in a vehicle whose sides are not designed and rated to contain such cargo.

(2) Pieces of rock weighing more than 100 kg (220 lb.), but less than 5,000 kg (11,000 lb.) must be secured, either in accordance with this section, or in accordance with the provisions of §§393.100 through 393.114, including:

(i) Rock contained within a vehicle which is designed to carry such cargo; or

(ii) Secured individually by tiedowns, provided each piece can be stabilized and adequately secured.

(3) Rock which has been formed or cut to a shape and which provides a stable base for securement must also be secured, either in accordance with the provisions of this section, or in accordance with the provisions of §§393.100 through 393.114.

(b) **General requirements for the positioning of boulders on the vehicle.** (1) Each boulder must be placed with its flattest and/or largest side down.

(2) Each boulder must be supported on at least two pieces of hard wood blocking at least 10 cm x 10 cm (4 inches x 4 inches) side dimensions extending the full width of the boulder.

(3) Hardwood blocking pieces must be placed as symmetrically as possible under the boulder and should support at least three-fourths of the length of the boulder.

(4) If the flattest side of a boulder is rounded or partially rounded, so that the boulder may roll, it must be placed in a crib made of hardwood timber fixed to the deck of the vehicle so that the boulder rests on both the deck and the timber, with at least three well-separated points of contact that prevent its tendency to roll in any direction.

(5) If a boulder is tapered, the narrowest end must point towards the front of the vehicle.

(c) **General tiedown requirements.** (1) Only chain may be used as tiedowns to secure large boulders.

4.3 Cargo Securement Regulations

(2) Tiedowns which are in direct contact with the boulder should, where possible, be located in valleys or notches across the top of the boulder, and must be arranged to prevent sliding across the rock surface.

(d) **Securement of a cubic shaped boulder.** In addition to the requirements of paragraphs (b) and (c) of this section, the following rules must be satisfied:

(1) Each boulder must be secured individually with at least two chain tiedowns placed transversely across the vehicle.

(2) The aggregate working load limit of the tiedowns must be at least half the weight of the boulder.

(3) The tiedowns must be placed as closely as possible to the wood blocking used to support the boulder.

(e) **Securement of a non-cubic shaped boulder-with a stable base.** In addition to the requirements of paragraphs (b) and (c) of this section, the following rules must be satisfied:

(1) The boulder must be secured individually with at least two chain tiedowns forming an "X" pattern over the boulder.

(2) The aggregate working load limit of the tiedowns must be at least half the weight of the boulder.

(3) The tiedowns must pass over the center of the boulder and must be attached to each other at the intersection by a shackle or other connecting device.

(f) **Securement of a non-cubic shaped boulder-with an unstable base.** In addition to the requirements of paragraphs (b) and (c) of this section, each boulder must be secured by a combination of chain tiedowns as follows:

(1) One chain must surround the top of the boulder (at a point between one-half and two-thirds of its height). The working load limit of the chain must be at least half the weight of the boulder.

(2) Four chains must be attached to the surrounding chain and the vehicle to form a blocking mechanism which prevents any horizontal movement. Each chain must have a working load limit of at least one- fourth the weight of the boulder. Whenever practicable, the angle of the chains must not exceed 45 degrees from the horizontal.

4.3 Cargo Securement Regulations

4.4 U.S. Manufacturing Standards

Tiedown assemblies and other attachment or fastening devices used to secure articles of cargo to, or in, commercial motor vehicles must conform to the following applicable standards:

Component	Standard
Steel Strapping[1,2]	Standard Specification for Strapping, Flat Steel and Seals, American Society for Testing and Materials (ASTM) D3953-97, February 1998.
Chain	National Association of Chain Manufacturers' Welded Steel Chain Specifications, September 28, 2005.
Webbing	Web Sling and Tiedown Association's Recommended Standard Specification for Synthetic Web Tiedowns, WSTDA-T1, 1998.
Wire Rope[3]	Wire Rope Technical Board's Wire Rope Users Manual, 2nd Edition, November 1985.
Cordage	Cordage Institute rope standard: (i) PETRS-2, Polyester Fiber Rope, 3-Strand and 8-Strand Constructions, January 1993; (ii) PPRS-2, Polypropylene Fiber Rope, 3-Strand and 8-Strand Constructions, August 1992; (iii) CRS-1, Polyester/Polypropylene Composite Rope Specifications, 3-Strand and 8-Strand Standard Construction, May 1979; (iv) NRS-1, Nylon Rope Specifications, 3-Strand and 8-Strand Standard Construction, May 1979; and (v) C-1, Double Braided Nylon Rope Specifications DBN, January 1984.

[1] Steel strapping not marked by the manufacturer with a working load limit will be considered to have a working load limit equal to one-fourth of the breaking strength listed in ASTM D3953-97.

[2] Steel strapping 25.4 mm (1 inch) or wider must have at least two pairs of crimps in each seal and, when an end-over-end lap joint is formed, must be sealed with at least two seals.

[3] Wire rope which is not marked by the manufacturer with a working load limit shall be considered to have a working load limit equal to one-fourth of the nominal strength listed in the manual.

4.4 U.S. Manufacturing Standards

Publisher Contacts

Underwriters Laboratories, Inc.
333 Pfingsten Road
Northbrook, Illinois 60062
www.ul.com
Ph: (847) 272-8800
Fax: (847) 272-8129

American Society for Testing and Materials
100 Barr Harbor Drive
West Conshohocken, Pennsylvania 19428-2959
www.astm.org
Ph: (610) 832-9500
Fax: (610) 832-9555

National Association of Chain Manufacturers
P.O. Box 89014
Tuscon, Arizona 85752
www.nacm.info
Ph: (520) 886-0695

Web Sling and Tiedown Association, Inc.
2105 Laurel Bush Rd., Suite 200
Bel Air, Maryland 21015
www.wstda.com
Ph: (443) 640-1070
Fax: (443) 640-1031

Wire Rope Technical Committee
P.O. Box 849
Stevensville, Maryland 21666

Cordage Institute
994 Old Eagle School Rd., Suite 1019
Wayne, Pennsylvania 19087
www.ropecord.com
Ph: (610) 971-4854
Fax: (610) 971-4859

4.5 Default Working Load Limits for Unmarked Tiedowns

Chain

Size in inches (mm)	WLL in pounds (kg)				
	Grade 30 proof coil	Grade 43 high test	Grade 70 transport	Grade 80 alloy	Grade 100 alloy
1/4 (7 mm)	1,300 (580* kg)	2,600 (1,180 kg)	3,150 (1,430 kg)	3,500 (1,570 kg)	4,300 (1,950 kg)
5/16 (8 mm)	1,900 (860 kg)	3,900 (1,770 kg)	4,700 (2,130 kg)	4,500 (2,000 kg)	5,700 (2,600 kg)
3/8 (10 mm)	2,650 (1,200 kg)	5,400 (2,450 kg)	6,600 (2,990 kg)	7,100 (3,200 kg)	8,800 (8,800 kg)
7/16 (11 mm)	3,700 (1,680* kg)	7,200 (3,270 kg)	8,750 (3,970 kg)	--	--
1/2 (13 mm)	4,500 (2,030* kg)	9,200 (9,200 kg)	11,300 (5,130 kg)	12,000 (5,400 kg)	15,000 (6,800 kg)
5/8 (16 mm)	6,900 (3,130 kg)	13,000 (5,910 kg)	15,800 (7,170 kg)	18,100 (8,200 kg)	22,600 (10,300 kg)
Chain mark examples:	3, 30, 300, G30, PC, C3, M3	4, 43, 430, G43, H, HT, M4, PH, C4, G4, G40	7, 70, 700, G70, G7, M7, C7	8, 80, 800, A8A, C8, TC8, CA8, G80	10, 100, 1000, W10, HA100, H26, P10, C10, A10, GC10

*Note: The Canadian Standard WLL for Grade 30 chain is 590 kg for 7 mm; 1,590 kg for 11 mm; and 2,040 kg for 13 mm.

For welded steel chain that is not marked with either the grade or working load limit, assume a working load limit equal to that for grade 30 proof coil.

4.5 Default Working Load Limits for Unmarked Tiedowns

Synthetic Webbing

Width in inches (mm)	WLL in pounds (kg)
1³/₄ (45 mm)	1,750 (790 kg)
2 (50 mm)	2,000 (910 kg)
3 (75 mm)	3,000 (1,360 kg)
4 (100 mm)	4,000 (1,810 kg)

Wire Rope
(6x37, Fiber Core)

Diameter in inches (mm)	WLL in pounds (kg)
1/4 (7 mm)	1,400 (640 kg)
5/16 (8 mm)	2,100 (950 kg)
3/8 (10 mm)	3,000 (1,360 kg)
7/16 (11 mm)	4,100 (1,860 kg)
1/2 (13 mm)	5,300 (2,400 kg)
5/8 (16 mm)	8,300 (3,770 kg)
3/4 (20 mm)	10,900 (4,940 kg)
7/8 (22 mm)	16,100 (7,300 kg)
1 (25 mm)	20,900 (9,480 kg)

Manila Rope

Diameter in inches (mm)	WLL in pounds (kg)
3/8 (10 mm)	205 (90 kg)
7/16 (11 mm)	265 (120 kg)
1/2 (13 mm)	315 (150 kg)
5/8 (16 mm)	465 (210 kg)
3/4 (20 mm)	640 (290 kg)
1 (25 mm)	1,050 (480 kg)

Propropylene Fiber Rope
(3-Strand and 8-Strand Construction)

Diameter in inches (mm)	WLL in pounds (kg)
3/8 (10 mm)	400 (180* kg)
7/16 (11 mm)	525 (240 kg)
1/2 (13 mm)	625 (280* kg)
5/8 (16 mm)	925 (420 kg)
3/4 (20 mm)	1,275 (580 kg)
1 (25 mm)	2,100 (950 kg)

*Note: The Canadian Standard WLL for synthetic fiber rope is 185 kg for 10 mm and 285 kg for 13 mm.

4.5 Default Working Load Limits for Unmarked Tiedowns

Polyester Fiber Rope
(3-Strand and 8-Strand Construction)

Diameter in inches (mm)	WLL in pounds (kg)
3/8 (10 mm)	555 (250 kg)
7/16 (11 mm)	750 (340 kg)
1/2 (13 mm)	960 (440 kg)
5/8 (16 mm)	1,500 (680 kg)
3/4 (20 mm)	1,880 (850 kg)
1 (25 mm)	3,300 (1,500 kg)

Nylon Rope

Diameter in inches (mm)	WLL in pounds (kg)
3/8 (10 mm)	278 (130 kg)
7/16 (11 mm)	410 (190 kg)
1/2 (13 mm)	525 (240 kg)
5/8 (16 mm)	935 (420 kg)
3/4 (20 mm)	1,420 (640 kg)
1 (25 mm)	2,520 (1,140 kg)

Double Braided Nylon Rope

Diameter in inches (mm)	WLL in pounds (kg)
3/8 (10 mm)	336 (150 kg)
7/16 (11 mm)	502 (230 kg)
1/2 (13 mm)	655 (300 kg)
5/8 (16 mm)	1,130 (510 kg)
3/4 (20 mm)	1,840 (830 kg)
1 (25 mm)	3,250 (1,470 kg)

Steel Strapping

Width x Thickness in inches (mm)	WLL in pounds (kg)
$1^{1}/_{4}$ x 0.029 (31.7 x 0.74 mm)	1,190 (540 kg)
$1^{1}/_{4}$ x 0.031 (31.7 x 0.79 mm)	1,190 (540 kg)
$1^{1}/_{4}$ x 0.035 (31.7 x 0.89 mm)	1,190 (540 kg)
$1^{1}/_{4}$ x 0.044 (31.7 x 1.12 mm)	1,690 (770 kg)
$1^{1}/_{4}$ x 0.05 (31.7 x 1.27 mm)	1,690 (770 kg)
$1^{1}/_{4}$ x 0.057 (31.7 x 1.5 mm)	1,925 (870 kg)
2 x 0.044 (50.8 x 1.12 mm)	2,650 (1,200 kg)
2 x 0.05 (50.8 x 1.27 mm)	2,650 (1,200 kg)

4.5 Default Working Load Limits for Unmarked Tiedowns

4.6 Tiedown Quick Reference

These charts indicate the minimum number* of indirect tiedowns (tiedowns with both ends attached to opposite sides of vehicle) needed to secure a load based only on the load's weight.

For direct tiedowns (tiedowns that are attached directly to the cargo or that have both tiedown ends attached to the same side of the vehicle), double the number of tiedowns shown. For welded steel chain that is not marked with either the grade or working load limit, assume a working load limit equal to that for grade 30 proof coil.

Chains

Grade of Chain	Size (in.)	Working Load Limit (lbs.)	Working Load Limit (kg.)	5,000 (2,268)	10,000 (4,536)	15,000 (6,804)	20,000 (9,072)	25,000 (11,340)	30,000 (13,608)	35,000 (15,876)	40,000 (18,144)	45,000 (20,412)	50,000 (22,680)
Grade 30 proof coil or unmarked	1/4	1,300	580	2	4	6	8	10	12	14	16	18	20
	5/16	1,900	860	2	3	4	6	7	8	10	11	12	14
	3/8	2,650	1,200	1	2	3	4	5	6	7	8	9	10
	7/16	3,700	1,680	1	2	3	3	4	5	5	6	7	7
Grade 43 high test	1/4	2,600	1,180	1	2	3	4	5	6	7	8	9	10
	5/16	3,900	1,769	1	2	2	3	4	4	5	6	6	7
	3/8	5,400	2,449	1	1	2	2	3	3	4	4	5	5
	7/16	7,200	3,270	1	1	2	2	2	3	3	3	4	4
Grade 70 transport	1/4	3,150	1,429	1	2	3	4	4	5	6	7	8	8
	5/16	4,700	2,132	1	2	2	3	3	4	4	5	5	6
	3/8	6,600	2,994	1	1	2	2	2	3	3	4	4	4
	7/16	8,750	3,970	1	1	1	2	2	2	2	3	3	3
Grade 80 alloy	1/4	3,500	1,570	1	2	3	3	4	5	5	6	7	8
	5/16	4,500	2,000	1	2	2	3	3	4	4	5	5	6
	3/8	7,100	3,200	1	1	2	2	2	3	3	3	4	4

*Note: Additional tiedowns may be needed based on the size of the load and/or your overall securement system. © 2006 J. J. Keller & Associates, Inc. 445-R-L (11699) (Rev. 8/06)

4.6 Tiedown Quick Reference

Synthetic Webbing

Width in Inches (mm)	Working Load Limit (lbs.)	Working Load Limit (kg.)	5,000 (2,268)	10,000 (4,536)	15,000 (6,804)	20,000 (9,072)	25,000 (11,340)	30,000 (13,608)	35,000 (15,876)	40,000 (18,144)	45,000 (20,412)	50,000 (22,680)
1-3/4 (45 mm)	1,750	790	2	3	5	6	8	9	10	12	13	15
2 (50 mm)	2,000	910	2	3	4	5	7	8	9	10	12	13
3 (75 mm)	3,000	1,360	1	2	3	4	5	5	6	7	8	9
4 (100 mm)	4,000	1,810	1	2	2	3	4	4	5	5	6	7

*Note: Additional tiedowns may be needed based on the size of the load and/or your overall securement system.

Wire Rope

Size in Inches (mm)	Working Load Limit (lbs.)	Working Load Limit (kg.)	5,000 (2,268)	10,000 (4,536)	15,000 (6,804)	20,000 (9,072)	25,000 (11,340)	30,000 (13,608)	35,000 (15,876)	40,000 (18,144)	45,000 (20,412)	50,000 (22,680)
1/4 (7 mm)	1,400	640	2	4	6	8	9	11	13	15	17	18
5/16 (8 mm)	2,100	950	2	3	4	5	6	8	9	10	11	12
3/8 (10 mm)	3,000	1,360	1	2	3	4	5	5	6	7	8	9
7/16 (11 mm)	4,100	1,860	1	2	2	3	4	4	5	5	6	7
1/2 (13 mm)	5,300	2,400	1	1	2	2	3	3	4	4	5	5
5/8 (16 mm)	8,300	3,770	1	1	1	2	2	2	3	3	3	4
3/4 (20 mm)	10,900	4,940	1	1	1	1	2	2	2	2	3	3
7/8 (22 mm)	16,100	7,300	1	1	1	1	1	1	2	2	2	2
1 (25 mm)	20,900	9,480	1	1	1	1	1	1	1	1	2	2

*Note: Additional tiedowns may be needed based on the size of the load and/or your overall securement system.

© 2006 J. J. Keller & Associates, Inc. 445-R-L (11699) (Rev. 8/06)

4.7 Glossary

A

Aggregate working load limit — The summation of the working load limits or restraining capacity of all devices used to secure an article on a vehicle.

Anchor point — Part of the structure, fitting, or attachment on a vehicle or cargo to which a tiedown is attached.

Article of cargo — A unit of cargo, other than a liquid, gas, or aggregate that lacks physical structure (e.g. grain, gravel, etc.), including articles grouped together so that they can be handled as a single unit or unitized by wrapping, strapping, banding, or edge protection device(s).

B

Banding — A strip of material that may be used to unitize articles and is tensioned and clamped or crimped back upon itself (same as "Strapping").

Bell pipe concrete — Pipe whose flanged end is of larger diameter than its barrel.

Binder — A device used to tension a tiedown or combination of tiedowns.

Blocking — A structure, device, or another substantial article placed against or around an article to prevent horizontal movement of the article.

Bolster — A transverse load bearing structural component, particularly a part of a log bunk.

Boulder — A large piece of natural rock that may be rounded if it has been exposed to weather and water, or is rough if it has been quarried.

Bracing — A structure, device, or another substantial article placed against an article to prevent it from tipping that may also prevent it from shifting.

Bulkhead — A vertical barrier across a vehicle to prevent forward movement of cargo.

4.7 Glossary

Bundle — A group of articles that has been unitized for securement as a single article.

Bunk — A horizontal bolster fitted with a stake at each end that together supports and contains a stack of logs, and is installed transversely.

Cab shield — A vertical barrier placed directly behind the cab of a tractor to protect the cab in the event cargo should shift forward.

Cargo — All articles or material carried by a vehicle, including those used in operation of the vehicle.

Chock — A tapered or wedge-shaped piece used to secure round articles against rolling.

Cleat — A short piece of material, usually wood, nailed to the deck to reinforce blocking.

Coil bunk — A device that keeps timbers supporting a metal coil in place.

Contained — Cargo is contained if it fills a sided vehicle, and every article is in contact with or sufficiently close to a wall or other articles so that it cannot shift or tip if those other articles are also unable to shift or tip.

Container chassis — A semitrailer of skeleton construction limited to a bottom frame, one or more axles, specially built and fitted with locking devices for the transport of cargo containers, so that when the chassis and container are assembled, the units serve the same function as an over-the-road trailer.

Container chassis vehicle — A vehicle especially built and fitted with locking devices for the transport of intermodal containers.

Cradle — A device or structure that holds a circular article to prevent it from rolling.

Crib-type log trailer means a trailer equipped with stakes, bunks, a front-end structure, and a rear structure to restrain logs. The stakes prevent movement of the logs from side to side on the vehicle while the front-end and rear structures

4.7 Glossary

prevent movement of the logs from front to back on the vehicle.

Crosswise — Same as "Lateral".

Crown — The rounded profile of the top of a stack of logs, when viewed from the ends of the stack.

Cut-to-length logs — Included in shortwood.

Deck — The load carrying area (floor or bed) of a truck, trailer, or intermodal container.

Direct tiedown — A tiedown that is intended to provide direct resistance to potential shift of an article.

Dunnage — All loose materials used to support and protect cargo.

Dunnage bag — An inflatable bag intended to fill otherwise empty space between articles of cargo, or between articles of cargo and the wall of the vehicle.

Edge protector — A device placed on the exposed edge of an article to distribute tiedown forces over a larger area of cargo than the tiedown itself, to protect the tiedown and/or cargo from damage, and to allow the tiedown to slide freely when being tensioned.

Eye (of a cylindrical object) — The hole through the center of the article.

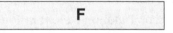

Flatbed vehicle — A vehicle with a deck but no permanent sides.

Frame vehicle — A vehicle with skeletal structure fitted with one or more bunk units for trans-

4.7 Glossary

porting logs. A bunk unit consists of a front bunk and a rear bunk that together cradle logs. The bunks are welded, gusseted, or otherwise firmly fastened to the vehicle's main beams, and are an integral part of the vehicle.

Friction mat — A device placed between the deck of a vehicle and cargo or between articles of cargo, intended to provide greater friction than exists naturally between these surfaces.

g — The acceleration due to gravity, 32.2 ft/sec^2 (9.823 m/sec^2).

Gross combination weight rating — The value specified for the vehicle by the manufacturer as being the maximum of the sum of the "gross vehicle mass" of the drawing vehicle plus the sum of the "axle loads" of all vehicles being drawn.

Gross vehicle weight rating — The maximum laden weight of a motor vehicle as specified by the manufacturer.

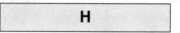

Headboard — A vertical barrier across the front of the deck of a vehicle to prevent forward movement of cargo.

Hook-lift container — A specialized container, primarily used to contain and transport materials in the waste, recycling, construction/demolition, and scrap industries, which are used in conjunction with specialized vehicles, in which the container is loaded and unloaded onto a tilt frame body by an articulating hook-arm.

4.7 Glossary

I

Indirect tiedown — A tiedown whose tension is intended to increase the pressure of an article or stack of articles on the deck of the vehicle.

Integral locking device — A device that is purposely designed and used to restrain an article of cargo on a vehicle by connecting and locking attachment point(s) on the article to anchor point(s) on the vehicle.

Integral securement system — A feature of roll-on/roll-off containers and hook-lift containers and their related transport vehicles in which compatible front and rear hold-down devices are mated to provide securement of the complete vehicle and its cargo.

Intermodal container — A reusable, transportable enclosure that is specially designed with integral locking devices that secure it to a container chassis trailer to facilitate the efficient and bulk shipping and transfer of goods by, or between various modes of transport, such as highway, rail, sea, and air.

J K L

Lateral — Sideways, transverse, crosswise, or across a vehicle.

Lengthwise — Same as "Longitudinal".

Lift — A tier of dressed timber, steel, or other materials.

Load binder — A binder incorporating an over-center locking action.

Load capacity — The weight of cargo that a vehicle can carry when loaded to its allowable gross vehicle weight in a particular jurisdiction.

Logs — Include all natural wood that retains the original shape of the bole of the tree, whether raw, partially, or fully processed. Raw logs include all tree species with bark that have been harvested and may have been trimmed or cut to

4.7 Glossary

some length. Partially processed logs that have been fully or partially debarked or further reduced in length. Fully processed logs include utility poles, treated poles, and log cabin building components.

Longitudinal — Lengthwise or along the length of a vehicle.

Longwood — All logs, including utility poles, that are not shortwood and are over 16 feet (4.9 m) long. Such logs are usually described as long logs or treelength.

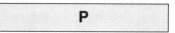

Metal coil means an article of cargo comprised of elements, mixtures, compounds, or alloys commonly known as metal, metal foil, metal leaf, forged metal, stamped metal, metal wire, metal rod, or metal chain that are packaged as a roll, coil, spool, wind, or wrap, including plastic or rubber coated electrical wire and communications cable. (U.S. only)

Pallet — A platform or tray on which cargo is placed so that it can be handled as an article (same as "Skid").

Pole Trailer — A trailer whose body consists simply of a drawbar by which the trailer is drawn.

Q R

Rail vehicle — A vehicle whose skeletal structure is fitted with stakes at the front and rear to contain logs loaded crosswise.

Restrained — An article that is not contained, but is prevented from tipping or shifting.

Rub rail — A rail along the side of a vehicle that protects the side of the vehicle from impacts.

4.7 Glossary

S

Secured — Contained or restrained.

Securing device — Any device specifically manufactured as a means to attach or secure cargo to a vehicle or trailer.

Shackle — A U-shaped metal coupling link closed by a bolt.

Shift — A change in the longitudinal or lateral position or orientation of an article.

Shoring bar — A structural section placed transversely between the walls of a vehicle to prevent cargo from tipping or shifting.

Shortwood — All logs typically up to 16 feet (4.9 m) long. Such logs are often described as cut-up logs, cut-to-length logs, bolts, or pulpwood. Shortwood may be loaded lengthwise or crosswise, though that loaded crosswise is usually no more than 102 inches (2.6 m) long.

Sided vehicle — A vehicle whose cargo compartment is enclosed on all four sides by walls of sufficient strength to contain cargo, where the walls may include latched openings for loading and unloading, and includes vans and dump bodies, and includes a sided intermodal container carried by a vehicle.

Skid — A platform or tray on which cargo is placed so that it can be handled as an article (same as "Pallet").

Spacer — Material placed beneath an article or between tiers of articles.

Stack — A single column of articles placed one above another.

Stack of logs — Logs aligned parallel and heaped one upon others.

Stake — A member mounted close to vertical on a vehicle frame or as part of a bunk that serves to immobilize cargo placed against it (same as "Standard").

4.7 Glossary

Stake pocket — A female housing fixed to the side or ends of a vehicle to receive a stake or peg, and may also be used as an anchor point.

Standard — A member mounted close to vertical on a vehicle frame or as part of a bunk that serves to immobilize cargo placed against it (same as "Stake").

Strapping — A strip of material that may be used to unitize articles and is tensioned and clamped or crimped back upon itself (same as "Banding").

T

Tarpaulin (tarp) — A waterproof sheet used to cover cargo.

Tension device — A device used to produce tension in a tiedown.

Tiedown — A combination of securing devices which form an assembly that attaches cargo to, or restrains cargo on, a vehicle or trailer, and is attached to anchor point(s).

Tiedown assembly — A combination of a tiedown with one or more tension devices that secures cargo to the vehicle on which it is being carried.

Tier — One layer of articles that are stacked one upon another.

Tip — An article falls over.

Track — A set of plates on a tractor wheel that provide mobility for a tracked vehicle.

Tractor-pole trailer — A vehicle that carries logs lengthwise so that they form the body of the vehicle. The logs are supported by a bunk located on the rear of the tractor and another bunk on the skeletal trailer. The bunks may rotate about a vertical axis, and the trailer may have a fixed, scoping, or cabled reach, or other mechanical freedom, to allow it to turn.

Transverse — Same as "Lateral".

4.7 Glossary

Twist lock — A device designed to support and fasten one corner of an intermodal container to a container chassis vehicle.

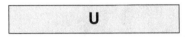

Unitized load — A number of articles grouped together with sufficient structural integrity that they can be handled, transported, and secured as a single article.

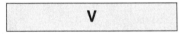

Vehicle — A truck, truck tractor, trailer, or semi-trailer individually or in combination.

Void filler — Material used to fill a void between articles of cargo and the structure of the vehicle that has sufficient strength to prevent movement of the articles of cargo.

Wedge — A tapered piece of material, thick at one end and thin at the other.

Well — The depression formed between two cylindrical articles when they are laid with their eyes horizontal and parallel against each other.

Winch — A device for tensioning a webbing or wire rope tiedown that is fitted with means to lock the initial tension.

Working load limit (WLL) — The maximum load that may be applied to a component of a cargo securement system during normal service, usually assigned by the manufacturer of the component.

X Y Z

4.7 Glossary